1970

LATIN POETRY
THE AGE OF RHETORIC AND SATIRE

LATIN POETRY

The Age of Rhetoric
and Satire

by

CLARENCE W. MENDELL

ARCHON BOOKS

1967

Library of Congress Catalog Card Number: 67-28320

Printed in the United States of America

Contents

Preface

THIS BOOK, like its predecessor, *Latin Poetry: The New Poets and the Augustans* (New Haven, 1965), is intended for the general reader who would like to revive a fading impression of poets with whom he once had at least a bowing acquaintance. In spite of the debt I necessarily owe to scholars past and present the interpretations are my own, as are the translations I have done in verse, hoping thereby to give some suggestion of the originals. Should the reader desire to know more about the poets he will find their complete works (so far as they are preserved) well edited and translated in the Loeb Classical Library, product of the Harvard University Press. If he finds a special interest in a particular poet he may find a complete—and probably overpowering—bibliography in M. Platnauer, *Fifty-Years of Classical Scholarship* (Oxford, 1955). For an account of the period covered here and its individual writers H. J. Rose, *A Handbook of Latin Literature* (3rd edit., London, 1958) is useful for reference, and J. Wight Duff, *A Literary History of Rome in the Silver Age* (3rd edit., New York, 1964) is a mine of information. H. E. Butler, *Post-Augustan Poetry from Seneca to Juvenal* (Oxford, 1909) is a more critical but also in some respects a more prejudiced guide. After nearly half a century J. W. Mackail, *Latin Literature* (rev. edit., New York, 1923) is still the most sympathetic and readable interpreter. For more special exploration of the individual poets the following suggestions may be useful.

PHAEDRUS and MANILIUS. These two transitional poets have been on the whole of minor interest to scholars and the general reader can only be referred to such literature as he may find dealing with Phaedrus' more famous source, Aesop. Manilius has become almost the private preserve of A. E. Housman whose work has been too technical and special to interest the amateur.

PERSIUS. The edition by John Conington edited by H. Nettleship

(3rd edit., Oxford, 1893) with a translation and commentary contains nearly all the information necessary about Persius. E. V. Arnold, *Roman Stoicism* (London, 1958) will furnish a good background.

LUCAN. The edition by Haskins and Heitland (London, 1887) provides all necessary information.

SENECA. Interest in Seneca's poetry has largely centered on the influence exerted by his tragedies on the drama of Elizabethan England. J. W. Cunliffe, *The Influence of Seneca on Elizabethan Tragedy* (Manchester, 1893, reprinted Hamden, 1965) collected the bulk of the evidence of direct influence. F. L. Lucas, *Seneca and Elizabethan Tragedy* (Cambridge, 1922) discusses the evidence. More comprehensive is C. W. Mendell, *Our Seneca* (New Haven, 1941, reprinted, Hamden, 1968) which also considers Seneca's tragedy as related to the Greek.

STATIUS, VALERIUS FLACCUS, SILIUS ITALICUS. Overshadowed by the national epic of Vergil, these three poets have not inspired any literature which will appeal to the general reader.

JUVENAL. The massive edition of J. E. B. Mayor (Macmillan, 1893) with a thousand pages of notes accompanying less than a a hundred of text, is a mine of information about innumerable matters many of them somewhat remote from Juvenal. The general reader may, with sufficient patience, be able to extract much of interest. He will also be greatly helped to an appreciation of Juvenal by reading Dr. Johnson's satires "London" and "The Vanity of Human Wishes".

MARTIAL. Gaston Boissier's "The Poet Martial" (in *Tacitus and Other Roman Studies,* New York, 1906) is not one of his most successful essays. He is inclined to patronize his subject. K. F. Smith, *Martial the Epigrammist and Other Essays* (Baltimore, 1920) is readable and appreciative.

RHETORIC AND SATIRE. Gaston Boissier, "The Schools of Declamation at Rome" (in *Tacitus and Other Roman Studies*) is Boissier at his best, but allowance must be made for his Gallic imagination. More pedestrian are E. P. Morris, *Horace: The Satires. With an Introduction and Notes* (New York, 1909) and C. W. Mendell, "Satire as Popular Philosophy" (*Classical Philology,* vol. 15, 1920).

LATIN POETRY
THE AGE OF RHETORIC AND SATIRE

CHAPTER ONE

The Age of Rhetoric and Satire

THE GOLDEN AGE of Augustus culminated in a decade of disappointment and gloom. Maecenas was gone and Vergil; Horace too, and Tibullus and Propertius. Of the brilliant literary lights who had given the age its aura of glory only Ovid remained, a thorn in the side of the princeps and a reminder to him of the failure of one part of his cherished restoration. Augustus' plans for choosing a successor had also gone awry and he looked with distrust on the possible influence of Tiberius, who was a choice of despair. It is doubtful whether Augustus ever really expressed sympathy for the Rome which he "left to be ground to bits by the grim Claudian jaws of Tiberius," but he certainly did all he could to establish some other successor. It cannot have been from any fear that his political plans would be foiled. Augustus must have known that Tiberius would not attempt any novelties in government. His was the conservative military type of mind which yearns for precedents to follow. It must rather have been the spirit in which he would follow precedent that worried Augustus. The older man may well have foreseen at least something of the grim system of espionage and suppression which was to replace his own method of maintaining the new government.

For, whatever may be the final judgment on the first two emperors, one thing is certain. Around the regime of Augustus there was an aura of optimism. The great Ara Pacis symbolised his central policy of peace and good will. Opponents and sceptics had been won over by all the arts of appeasement. Public enthusiasm had been cultivated by means of slightly camouflaged doles, great games and public pageants and a flamboyant building program.

The conservative doubters were lured by the official doctrines of economy and the Roman equivalent of Puritanism. The intellectuals were brought into the fold by the systematic encouragement of literature that merged the best culture of Greece with the rugged nationalism of Rome. Such exceptions as there were to universal peace were on the far frontiers, victories of Roman arms over barbarians beyond the pale won almost exclusively by the prestige of Roman regulars and the sacrifice of non-Roman auxiliaries, victories to be celebrated at Rome with holidays and public merrymaking. Whatever may have been the personal philosophy of Augustus, his public policy for the capitol of the world was unquestionably the creation of a popular spirit of optimistic enthusiasm. Perhaps if a Drusus or a Germanicus could have succeeded the first emperor the spirit of his creation might have lived.

There is no evidence to be found of any optimistic spirit of gladness in Rome for many years after the accession of Tiberius. A specious flash, soon extinguished, in the early days of Nero, a moment of hope under Vespasian. Otherwise, nearly a century of grim one-party government supported by force or the threat of force. A vast amount of investigation has been devoted to the government of the early empire in an effort to understand its routine and method and to determine whether and to what extent it was an absolute tyranny. It has come to be generally believed that the provinces were happier and better governed than they had been under the republic and of this there can be little question. The system of Augustus, further centralized into an efficient bureaucracy under Claudius, gave a stability to the provincials from Spain to Syria that was new. No matter who was emperor, the provincial government continued to function reasonably well, and even when revolution originated in a province it was the army there and not the provincials that sought a change of emperor. The citizens of the provinces were content with good government, reasonable justice and excellent business. The greatest profits from the business undoubtedly flowed toward Rome to swell the fortunes of wealthy freedmen and privileged favorites and to add to the scandalous luxury that raised a satiric protest throughout the century. But the provinces were prosperous; many provincials were rich and not a few came to Rome to spend their fortunes.

At Rome the picture was not the same. While it was from Rome that the one-party tyranny operated, also at Rome it found its most powerful opposition and at Rome it produced the least contentment and satisfaction. This is not particularly surprising. In most of the provinces the Roman Empire simply replaced other forms of absolute power and the imperial government was less oppressive than these had been, offered greater privileges, and usually raised the general standard of living. There were no vestiges of rebellion, save now and then in Gaul and Britain. And these provinces did not feel any oppressive tyranny but rather welcomed the possibilities of peaceful trade and transportation. Only in Judaea where dissatisfaction was an ingrained national trait was there chronic unhappiness.

But at Rome were concentrated a dozen sources of hatred and opposition. A limited number of aristocratic conservatives still cherished a nostalgic passion for the old regime of the Republic. While Augustus lived they had been temporarily under the effect of his sedatives but Tiberius offered no palliatives with the dose of monarchy. The survivors of the old senatorial party must have realised that the Republic was no longer a living possibility. It had been ailing for a century. It died forever when the mob followed Caesar to his burial and failed to support the tyrannicides. Its sponsors, however, could always point to the great days of old and they never failed to fling in the face of imperial usurpers the taunt of newness and charges of wanton luxury that had the specious but telling ring of righteousness. These came more and more to be a political gesture. The "Republicans" had the nuisance value of the French Royalists but little more.

Many of the men who liked to figure in this worship of a forgotten chivalry were also to be found in more active opposition. It was not a long step from the sentimental dislike of the system to personal hostility toward the figure who headed the system. Many a republican was willing to waive his sturdy republicanism if the opportunity were offered him to purify the throne by occupying it. Rome was rarely free from intrigue, plots or even incipient revolution which sought to displace one emperor and enthrone another on what were always presented as patriotic grounds. There were personal court feuds too, intrigues which featured Agrippina and Poppaea and a whole parade of mothers, wives and mistresses who sought control of the hand that guided the state.

All this sort of potential or real opposition to the current administration involved the aristocratic group. Few enough of its members could trace their prestige back to the senatorial families of the Republic. Civil war and proscription had largely wiped out these families so that the longest pedigrees reached only to the appointees of Augustus. Newcomers, however, were loud in their claims to aristocratic prestige and the emperors knew well the importance of maintaining this class consciousness. Nevertheless, the real strength of the new regime lay not in the socially distinguished but in the more practically competent group that filled the offices directly dependent on the emperor rather than on the senate. This class consisted largely of freedmen. The fact that Roman slaves had always been in the mass prisoners of war taken from nations with much longer traditions of culture than those of Rome, together with the fact that manumission in one form or another was sure to come to an intelligent slave in the course of a comparatively few years, resulted in a large and growing class of freedmen not wholly unlike today's middle class bourgeoisie. The most prominent among the class were likely to be of Greek origin. The great bulk of Roman business was in the hands of the freedmen; they conducted the clerical work of all officialdom whether financial, legal or administrative; theirs were the important portfolios in the bureaucracy of the empire. The "nobility" was a fading minority even while the name of Caesar still had power with the masses. The freedman class was in the saddle certainly from the days of Claudius on. From this group there could be little fear of any republican revolution; its interests were best served by a centralised monarchy. Yet there lay on this group no conservative restraint deriving from tradition or respect for the past. For them the past did not exist. They lived for the present and the future, for themselves and not for Rome, for what they could make out of any situation. From this group there would come no consistent class opposition, no ideological threats, but also from it each emperor gained his strongest support and faced an unlimited variety of rivalries and conspiracies.

As the century advanced, the danger of military opposition grew more obvious. To be sure, the empire had been founded on military force: the armies of Caesar and Pompey had split the Roman world and each new emperor sought the support of the praetorians more anxiously than that of the senate. But this background of force had been camouflaged by Augustus and polite fiction kept it from being too evident until the year of the four emperors tore the fiction to shreds and showed that any army might make an emperor. The Praetorian Guard, the emperor's own picked troops stationed close at hand, became more obviously the background of his immediate power but at the same time the most obvious source of open revolution if successfully tampered with.

The rabble of Rome, dependent in large part on the favor of the throne, was hardly an immediately potential opposition. It could and undoubtedly did grumble if doles were insufficient and amusements too few or lacking in novelty. But it was a rabble without intelligence and without any memories of lost liberty to give it coherence. It could be roused by a demagogue to play the chorus in some great political drama but it was not yet a leading character.

This superficial survey by no means exhausts the possibilities of opposition to the one-party government at Rome. There were business interests that might at any time conflict with imperial policies, there were substantial provincials who moved to Rome and resented the display of luxury, bad taste and immorality which too often surrounded the court, and there were doubtless innumerable hatreds such as a government without the counterweight of a legitimate opposition always breeds. And no emperor had taken the final step to insure his tyranny: there was no effective, ruthless secret police, no thorough purge of the opposition. Roman tradition never suffered this last humiliation to crush the genius of free Rome. This statement may seem at first glance ridiculous in view of all that has been written about the delators and their filthy trade. But delation was a private enterprise, not a government function, and the elimination of individuals was still dependent on the forms at least of judicial procedure or on individual assassination. The procedure was clumsy and liable to failure. Hence the uncertainty which explains a great part of the unhappiness pervading much of the literature of the first century. The men who profited by the regime, who manned the government bureaus and conducted the business of the world, were not men of letters. The literature which has come down to us was produced by men who were actually or potentially in opposition to the one-party absolutism of the empire. And the literature represents the spirit, not of the empire but of the city of Rome, where all alike, whether with the government or against it, lived in an atmosphere of uncertainty. Symptomatic of the condition is the fact that this was the heyday of the soothsayer and fortune teller, the century which saw the popularity of the exotic and often licentious religions of Egypt and Syria among the middle and upper classes while the poor turned to the penitential religions which offered a hope of future reward. The intellectual, as unhappy as the illiterate, turned to philosophy and sought to console himself with the cold comfort of Stoicism or the warmer refuge of Epicurean materialism. The great unifying religion of national faith was long since gone. Under the one-party government each man was left to make his own peace with life in a grim atmosphere of uncertainty.

All this is undoubtedly over-simplified and in part exaggerated. But it will perhaps make more comprehensible the tendencies which dominate beyond question the first century after Christ. These are, first, a general loss of that creative urge which led the Augustan poets to add new areas to the field of Latin literature, drawing their inspiration from the best Greek prototypes but always infused with a national enthusiasm. In the second place, there are two contrasted tendencies, one to withdraw from reality and, with a total disregard of the affairs of the day, to elaborate the artificial appeal of outward form; the other, with complete awareness of the immediate realities, to criticise, insofar as that was possible, the life and politics, the manners and morals of the day.

It might seem under these circumstances that the transition from Augustus to Tiberius would probably be accompanied by a cessation in the output of literature. At first glance there in fact appears to have been a sterile period so far as poetry is concerned. Ovid did not die until 18 A.D. but his great work had been completed many years before. Phaedrus and Manilius who lived and wrote well on into the days of Tiberius represent only a feeble afterglow of the Golden Age. Not until Nero's time do we come upon poets of distinction whose work has survived. These obvious facts are, however, somewhat misleading. There was not, in the field of poetry, "the silence of the graveyard" but the continuous and clamorous din of the recitation platform. Poetry was fashionable, that is, poetry of a sort. Tiberius himself set the fashion of writing verse and surrounded himself with young poets. Horace knew and seems to have encouraged a number of younger poets. The Ars Poetica was written ostensibly to guide the young Pisos in their efforts to write tragedy. In Epist. I.3 to Julius Florus Horace seeks information about the literary activity of four young friends who are accompanying Tiberius on a campaign in the East. He raises the question prominent in the opening odes of Book IV: which of you young poets is going to write the epic of Augustus? Ovid's register of poets (Ex Pont. IV.16) presents more than a score of versifiers, lyric, epigrammatic, elegiac, epic, dramatic, whose lives covered a long span of years extending well into the reign of Tiberius. But the product of their efforts which has for the most part vanished was definitely different from the Augustan output and certainly not qualified for immortality.

One fact is reasonably sure. From the end of the Augustan Age Roman poets almost unanimously cease going back, either actually or ostensibly, to Greek models and accept Vergil and Horace and the elegiac trio as their progenitors. After Phaedrus and Manilius we hear of no attempts to add new types to the body of Roman poetry or to Romanize more Greek poetic types. Only in the case of Calpurnius perhaps is the imitation of the Augustan poets servile but, in spite of a complete change of spirit and purpose in each case, Lucan and the other epic writers looked back to Vergil as their prototype, while Persius and Juvenal went straight to Horace. The lost elegiac poets and dramatists seem largely to have modeled themselves on Ovid. Seneca's tragedies have little kinship with the Greek plays beyond the myths with which they dealt and these had been already appropriated by Roman writers.

RHETORIC

The most outstanding influence discernible in the literature of the first century, largely determining its character, is what has been generally recognized as the rhetorical element. But this term has been so widely and often so carelessly used as to lose some of its meaning and force. It is of enough importance to warrant careful consideration.

As a matter of fact, rhetorical influence was concrete and specific, general only in the sense of being wide-spread. The root of the later growth, like so many roots of things Roman, lies in Greek soil. First in Sicily, when the tyrants had been eliminated, and then in Athens, when her great days were fading into a memory, the practical politics of vocal democracies made the art of persuasion an asset of prime importance. Characteristically enough, the first practical teacher of rhetoric was, so tradition tells us, a man who had himself failed in practical politics, Corax of Sicily. He first, and a little after him Gorgias, gave exhibitions and lessons and distributed textbooks in Athens at the end of the fifth century. The two professed to teach men how to make speeches which would persuade the hearers on any subject and on either side. They laid down principles of diction and arrangement and methods of creating an atmosphere of probability. This of course, for they were by no means lacking in shrewdness, included means of pleasing the audience as a step towards persuading it. It was the stress laid on persuasion as opposed to truth which made Plato the bitter enemy of these sophists as they were called.

Their method of teaching consisted largely in the assumption of general propositions or of specific hypothetical cases and then in either speaking to the question by way of example or of listening to and criticizing the speeches made by their pupils.

All of this applied first and chiefly to the art of the orator. Aristotle summed up the doctrine but, with his passion for logic, he transferred the emphasis. His three great divisions of the subject were proofs, arrangement and delivery; the true sophist cared little for the proofs. Aristotle also introduced the age-long argument on styles which need not enter here to confuse the issue. We are concerned only with the distinction which Theophrastus makes clear between a style which looks to the facts, the concern of the philosopher, and a style which looks to the hearer, rhetoric proper.

The art of persuasive speaking had many generations for development in the Greek world before it came to Rome. It came there first in the form of a quarrel between styles and so it appears in Cicero's day. Which is more persuasive, a simple or an ornate style? The earlier Romans had had but the vaguest idea of artistic construction. Crude treatises had begun to circulate, but not until a situation like that following the Gracchan revolution made it personally profitable for the orator to sway his audience. Cicero himself, while wary of the extremely ornate style, never questioned the necessity for an art and a training and chose to temper his eloquence only because he was convinced that it thus became more persuasive. An oration is to him distinct in style from what he calls *sermo*, the style of philosophy whose concern is truth. All of this was, in Cicero's day, confined to the professionals. The treatise was a textbook for the would-be orator; the controversies over style were the arguments between specialists; such declaiming as existed was merely the practice of the professional lawyer at his own home. But the time was soon to come when the words of an orator could no longer go far toward influencing policy. Before the Empire had discarded its swaddling clothes the great day of oratory had passed, though the technique of the orator's training lived on to appear in a new and ominous incarnation.

The expansion of the influence of rhetoric was possible because the teaching of the rhetor's school, designed to train public speakers, was the training of *all* educated men. When oratory ceased to have practical importance because of the development of one-man power and the disappearance of an authoritative forum for the orator, the influence of the training became obvious in other lines of endeavor to which the educated man turned. The published case books of the elder Seneca, one of the ablest of the rhetorical teachers, give us a definite idea of the process. Seneca was old enough to have heard Cicero and died late in the reign of Tiberius. He was therefore conversant with the whole development. This development was in brief the establishment of the *declamatio* or public recitation of literary productions of every type. It began with the declamation of speeches on hypothetical cases, often highly fanciful and complex, ostensibly to train the young speaker but at the same time furnishing him the opportunity of exhibiting his oratorical wares. These declamations, Seneca definitely states, were modern; in his youth no orator gave public recitations. When the public began to be admitted an essential change was inevitable. In the introductory epistle to Book III of the *Controversiae*, Seneca makes a sharp distinction between declaiming and speaking in court, between appealing to an audience and to a judge. The former is *supervacua* and he compares it with toiling in one's dreams. He still has in mind that at that period boys and young men, eager to learn, comprised the bulk at least of the audience when a lawyer of any note declaimed. Such an audience was not unlikely to be a temptation to show off.

It was Asinius Pollio, in the time of Augustus, who according to Seneca first read or recited what he had written to an invited audience though *numquam admissa multitudine declamavit*. Haterius invited the mob even to his extemporeaneous efforts and the fat was in the fire. The key to the change is to be found in a remark in Seneca's introduction to his ninth book of the *Controversiae*: "Montanus Votienus went so far in refusing to make a show of declaiming that he did not declaim even for practice"; and his reason was: "He who composes a declamation writes not to win a case but to please." So Labienus had already scorned recitations not only, as Seneca somewhat naively says, because the institution had not yet been invented but because he considered it a disgraceful and frivolous exhibition. But Montanus and Labienus seem to have been exceptions to the rule. Seneca's collection bears witness to the considerable number of orators who exhibted their wares before audiences at recitations. It did not take the poets long to follow a custom which gave them a chance to try out their literary creations.

The audiences at the recitations consisted of the people who formed the new society of post-Augustan Rome, increasingly in a hurry over nothing, increasingly superficial, increasingly jaded in the nerves and ever more eager for speed, novelty, excitement of any kind. In fact, not very different from society in our own day. In the days of Augustus society had still consisted in large part of those who, by inheritance and opportunity, had some real background of culture and of those who, by real worth, had earned their place alongside the scions of the older stock. But the following century saw a steadily increasing proportion of intruders within the sacred portals of society. Even if we largely discount the attacks of philosophers, satirists and wits it is obvious that money was the best passport into the desired realm and aggressive obsequiousness the best weapon of assault. The nouveau riche and the clamorous upstart were in all likelihood the most patient and appreciative listeners at the average recitation. It is undoubtedly true that there were readings like those of the younger Pliny at a much later date which were given for the sake of getting real criticism but these were exceedingly rare. Even Pliny was aware of the more common kind of reading at which the interest of the audience was calculated.

We have a graphic if satirical description of a recitation in the first satire of Persius. It presents a scene which would have been impossible in the days of Horace when a poet was forced to corner a listener at the baths in order to get a hearing. In Persius' satire the reader appears dressed up in his best finery, gargles his throat, rolls his eyes and pours forth rippling measures which enthrall his audience. Such a scene the poet declares is not uncommon. The world of Rome is all agog for the latest poem and there is no dearth of producers; *scribimus inclusi, numero ille, hic pede liber, grande aliquid quod pulmo animae praelargus anhelet.* However much he exaggerates, Persius certainly did not *imagine* the scene. Neither can this fully developed recitation custom have sprung up spontaneously. Persius died in 62 A.D. and the custom which he satirizes in its full bloom must have been developing long before the reign of Nero. Such literary readings were called *recitationes* in distinction from the legal *declamationes*. They created a convenient form of publication but a dangerous one. It looked toward the approval of a social group scarcely qualified to render sound literary criticism and often disqualified by the fact that the listeners themselves were more than likely to be the performers on a later occasion. It lent authority to oral effects, to superficial, perhaps temporary, often specious attractions, almost anything to hold attention. It also limited the scope, both in quality and in quantity, of effective production to what a socially constituted audience could cheerfully absorb at a sitting.

The particular means for attracting and holding an audience's attention as taught by the rhetors and practiced by the poets were various. Prominent among them were striking antitheses, anaphora, vivid description, dramatic narrative, emotional exaggeration and sententious, epigrammatic phrases. The last item was one of the most eagerly strained after. Seneca describes his fellow pupil, Porcius Latro, as spending whole days writing those *translaticias quae sententias dicimus, quae nihil habent cum ipsa controversia implicitum, sed apte et alio transferuntur*. These commonplaces are *de fortuna, de crudelitate, de saeculo, de divitiis*. Such was the material which the young student gathered to stock his armory and these four topics came from the Stoics, whether in serious philosophical essays or in the more popular Satire or merely from the general fund of everyday proverbial wisdom. For the Roman popular ethics was Stoic in the same sense as that in which we speak of our western civilization as Christian. The most universally accepted commonplace and at the same time probably the least honored in practice was that money was the root of nearly all evil. Seneca dates the demise of oratory from the influx of luxury with its accompanying evils: sloth, the passion for singing and dancing, effeminacy, immorality. To Horace money was the greatest source of evil as it was later to Juvenal. Tacitus, in the *Dialogus*, agrees with Seneca on the beginning of the decline of real oratory. Orthodoxy agreed with the policy of the government rather than with its practice.

It is at this level of the quotable maxim that the rhetorical training meets on common ground the tradition of Roman Satire, the most distinctly original product of Roman literary genius and the second of the major influences on the output of the first century.

SATIRE

When Quintilian said "Satire is wholly ours" he might, with the same approximation to the truth, have added that by his day Satire had permeated all Roman literature. It was not only as a literary type that Satire was purely Roman. The spirit of Satire in its complex unity was essentially a Roman spirit, caustic, humorous, colloquial, critical and picturesque. The spirit antedates the type. When the name Satire came into use as a literary term, probably in the Augustan Age, the critics promptly applied it in retrospect to much earlier writing which showed the same essential characteristics as the satires of Horace. Horace himself looked to Lucilius as his prototype but the name soon attached itself to products of Ennius' pen as well. Eventually such diverse compositions as those of Varro and those of Juvenal were alike called Satire. Divergent as they were in form they were alike in the spirit which informed them. The original implication of the name, that of a miscellaneous, catch-all type of literature, gave way to a connotation of caustic and humorous criticism with an implicit moral purpose. This moral intent might be obscured by the urbanity or by the indignation of the writer but it was always implicit in the observations of a Horace or the fulminations of a Juvenal. And it was in the character of moral and social critic and reformer that the satirist extended his influence over the writers of other types of literature.

It is in the first century of our era that the adverse criticism of contemporary life becomes most insistent. It may be that we have lost a mass of literature which showed only satisfaction with the contemporary scene, which gloried in the advance of civilization and the increase of public magnificence and private luxury, which eulogised the empire as the triumph of modernism over the antiquated ideas of the republic. But the members of a newly rich society involved in an unfamiliar social ease, trying out every possible avenue to pleasure without the restraint imposed by a traditionally Puritanic culture, are not likely to burst into literature. The literary output of the age as it has come down to us from the days of Tiberius to those of Hadrian is almost wholly on the pessimistic side and presents life as somehow spoiled by the race for wealth, the scramble for social prestige, the loss of character and the failure of free institutions.

In the literature which has survived to our day there is no indication that the Romans were at all concerned about the national character before the time of the so-called Scipionic Circle. In the early days the simple duties of a citizen occupied his full time and duty to the state comprised the whole duty of man. But in the second century before Christ came great changes. Velleius Paterculus (II.1.1) states categorically: *Potentiae Romanorum prior Scipio viam aperuerat, luxuriae posterior aperuit*. And he follows this statement with a conclusion which he does not consider open to argument and which none of the critics of his day seems to have questioned: *a virtute descitum, ad vitia transcursum*. To Sallust, the destruction of Carthage opened the world to Rome's ambition for power and gave her access to the luxuries which destroyed her character. He uses the familiar terms of Stoic philosophy in such abundance as to remind us that it was the very Scipio who destroyed Carthage and so opened the floodgates to luxury who also gathered about himself the distinguished group of writers and scholars who forged the weapons, philosophical and literary, with which to flay that luxury.

For what Puritanism was to do for a later age Stoicism did for Rome. It furnished first a dogma supporting a rather grim school of thought in opposition to the trend of the times, a dogma maintained seriously and, by many of its adherents, fanatically. But, in its second and somewhat softened phase, Stoicism provided an almost universally accepted point of view and with it the vocabulary for criticism of all who were not, at least professedly, believers in the creed. As it came to Rome, largely through the more urbane interpretations of Panaetius, Stoicism was the philosophy which most nearly expressed the early Roman ideals of simple courage, thrift, loyalty and patriotism. There was enough in common between the Roman concept of *virtus* and the Stoic to make possible an identification and an absorption comparable with the acceptance of Greek gods as the equivalent of their nearest Roman counterparts. When Cato and his like could not exclude or banish Greek Philosophy, the Romans followed their usual policy and gradually absorbed and made their own whatever in it was least strange to them.

In this second phase Stoicism was at Rome reduced in scope so that for the average man it was largely a code of decent behavior based on a series of maxims which could be applied to the practical affairs of life. The serious scholar of Cicero's type might be interested in the theory of Stoic doctrine; for the average man it consisted of a series of wise saws which he approved with little thought and without necessarily putting them into practice.

The position attained by Stoicism at an early period may be readily realized by a glance at the position of its rival philosophy, Epicureanism. With its more intricate, intellectual basis of thought the school of Epicurus became the minority opposition to the orthodox Stoicism. To the latter it was something like the "scientific spirit" of modern times in its relation to religious conviction. There was not complete antagonism. Seneca, the Stoic, could make Epicurus his chief source of quotation but he was using what he considered good from the storehouse of his adversary. The enlightened Epicurean was as good a man as the sincere Stoic and usually a pleasanter one. He was apt to be an intellectual aristocrat. But the Stoic could easily misrepresent the Epicurean position and the unreasoning common man was quick to seize on a theory which he did not understand—but which he could lightly define as "eat, drink and be merry"—as a sanction for rejecting what appeared the more exacting moral requirements of Stoicism. He did this, however, in a sort of defiance of accepted standard, not as a reasoned way of life which he could defend. In general, Stoicism became the accepted code of Rome in much the same sense as Christianity is to-day the accepted code of the western world. Its chief concern was determined by the circumstances of the time exactly as is that of every religion which undertakes to guide the behavior of masses of men.

Lucilius was the first writer we know of to express in metrical form a protest against the cardinal vices which were the target of the Stoic preachers, and in his day, of these cardinal vices, it was luxury which was most in evidence. What Lucilius wrote seems to have been of the most miscellaneous character. Scholarship has

still much to discover about the background as well as the form
and content of that product. We know from Horace and the rest
that he arraigned the leaders and the mass in no measured terms,
that he revealed his own character clearly and fully; we know
from the fragments and the commentators that he wrote on ban-
quets and morals and linguistic usage; we know that he used
various meters with the hexameter winning the day. Furthermore,
and these are the most important items for the present discussion,
we know that "he was the friend of virtue only" and that at least
one book of his *Sermones* was an attack on wealth and the wealthy.
Finally we know without the shadow of a doubt that Horace
looked upon Lucilius as the originator of the kind of thing he wrote
and came to call Satire and that he and the rest of Rome's literary
clique were sufficiently sure of this relationship to apply the term
Satire to Lucilius' verses. He was taken for granted as a sincere
and outspoken Stoic, expressing himself in unpoetic verse of a
sufficiently urbane character to be acceptable and yet free from any
charge of artificial polish. In a self-conscious way he sought to
reproduce the homely wit and wisdom of an Ofellus as Benjamin
Franklin might travel in the guise of poor Richard.

Along with Lucilius others passed on the commonplaces which
represented to the average Roman the teaching of the Stoa. These
appeared to some extent in the plays of Terence, too polished to be
popular on the holiday stage which was devoted to the school of
Plautus but avidly read by the culture seeking litterati because of
their Greek atmosphere and strict Latinity. Cicero expounded the
teaching in more didactic form calculated to furnish useful material
to the orator who felt the need of giving a sound moral tone to the
color of his speeches. And Varro, the research scholar, went back
of the urbane missionary of Stoicism to a source nearer to the
fountainhead and reproduced in Latin the *Pseudogeloion* of Menip-
pus in the hybrid Satire of prose and verse mixed which some
called *Menippeia*, some *Cynica*. Undoubtedly there were others
but these we know and these were presumably the important
factors in molding and perpetuating the conventional, stereotyped
morality of Roman literature.

In the hands of Horace, Satire developed rapidly from its

harsher forms into an urbane and genial critique of the contemporary scene. But its fundamental characteristics remained the same: attack on the cardinal vices of luxury, avarice, superstition and lust, of which the greatest was luxury; assumption of an easy colloquialism, caustic wit and urbane irony; support of a theory of social obligation and patriotic duty. In the atmosphere of the Augustan Age the earlier bitterness largely disappeared, but the vehicle of expression was at hand for use by a later age and the spirit of satiric criticism remained to permeate its literature.

CHAPTER TWO

Phaedrus

THE FABLE has never attained high standing in the literature of any country. Stemming from primitive folk-lore, it may furnish homely illustration for more dignified types of writing but in general we are inclined to associate it with children's books. In western culture the beast fable in its origin is inseparable from the name of Aesop, supposed to have been a Phrygian slave liberated by his Samian master at some time not far from 600 B.C. Two hundred years later a statue by Lysippus was raised in Athens to the eastern slave. It may well be that the tradition that Aesop was a slave derived from the humble nature of his literary contribution. Nothing which he wrote has, to our certain knowledge, survived. Gradually all traditional fables, naturally anonymous, were ascribed to him and in the library at Alexandria Demetrius of Phaleron, a contemporary of Lysippus, collected them for the first time. Hence arises an Aesopic Question, a small relative of the Homeric Question: was Aesop written by Aesop or by another man of the same name? Or was there never an Aesop at all? From the collection of Demetrius, a humble writer of the time of Christ named Phaedrus made a volume of fables in Latin verse, most of which he ascribed to Aesop as their inventor. But between Aesop and Phaedrus a great deal had happened in the literary world.

Roman literature had begun, something over a hundred years after Demetrius, with a translation of Homer's Odyssey into Latin accentual verse and continued for nearly two centuries to consist mainly of translations, adaptations and imitations of Greek epic and drama. The drama was written by freedmen and others definitely below the salt to gain a living through sale to the aediles for performance at the Roman festivals. The epic was written under semi-official patronage on the part of leaders in the state to lend distinction to the history of Rome. Not until 100 B.C., when conquest and trade had extended and enriched the republic so that men of the governing class had the education and leisure to interest themselves in poetry, was the first real native product developed. This statement is not strictly true. Native Roman characteristics had always been evident in the adaptations from the Greek. The fervor and impressive dignity of Ennius and the riotous gaiety of Plautus were truly Roman, but the products which exhibited these qualities were traditional in form and essentially Greek. No Roman poet had as yet conceived of poetry as a vehicle for the direct expression of his own emotions and ideas.

Lucilius first broke the ice with essays in verse on a great miscellany of subjects but without any pretence of poetic beauty either of form or sentiment. It was Catullus and a group of young poets, during a period of violent social and political change, who declared their independence of tradition and began to express their emotions of love and hate with passion and often with great poetic beauty. Because they also imitated the academic school of Alexandria and wrote complicated and somewhat learned narrative poetry and also erotic elegies about extra-marital love experiences, they were considered by Horace and his followers as less than admirable. They did however revolutionize Roman poetry and pave the way for Horace and Vergil and Ovid. Vergil's dramatic epic was a truly Roman product in spite of the debt which he freely acknowledged to Homer, and Horace, paying homage to Archilochus and Sappho and Alcaeus, is one hundred per cent Roman.

By the time of Tiberius Roman literature had absorbed and Romanized the epic, the lyric, the epode, the erotic elegy, the epyllion and the epigram and had made its own contribution, the satire. Each poet prided himself on adding to the types of Roman literature. Born too late for the inspiring atmosphere of the Augustan Age, a foreigner by birth and a humble ex-slave as well, Phaedrus nevertheless had the ambition to add one more to the poetic conquests of Rome. The fable was about all that was left and the fable was within the range of his ability.

Phaedrus, in spite of his limited genius, knew something of the poets who preceded him and had the desire if not the ability to rival them. Admitting that his Muse was a slender one, he claimed to have added one more to the fields of poetry in which Rome could challenge Greece. When he wrote the prologue to his first book he must surely have been thinking of Horace's *Exegi monumentum*, if not of Lucretius' claim to a crown from the Muses or even of those discarded lines which were to have opened the *Aeneid* of Vergil. The prologue is short and modest. Phaedrus had no patron to address and so spoke to the general public.

> Aesop it was who first conceived these tales:
> I turned them out in our sennarian verse.
> The volume brings two gifts: 'twill make you smile
> And bring you good advice to guide your life.
> But if you cavil at the circumstance
> That trees are made to talk and beasts as well,
> Remember, these are made up fairy tales.

It seems probable that his books were published separately. They show an increasing assurance on the part of the writer and an increasing range of subject matter. The second, still addressed to the general reader, has a longer and slightly more confident prologue and contains one fable based on a contemporary incident. It closes with an epilogue which shows considerable self-confidence.

> The men of Athens raised a marble shaft
> To Aesop—public tribute to a slave—
> To prove that paths to fame are free to all
> And glory stems from virtue not from birth.
> So, since another bars my being first,
> I've striven ('tis all that's left) to equal him.
> Not envy this but honest rivalry.
> And so, if Latium smiles upon my toil,
> She shall have something more to match with Greece.
> If jealous scorn attack my honest best

It cannot spoil my joy in work well done.
If then my efforts come to cultured ears
That sense the art in these my fairy tales
My happiness shall banish all complaint.
But, should my artful labor meet with those
Whom nature brought to life in evil mood,
I shall endure my fate with heart of oak
Till Fortune blush at her misguided stroke.

The third book is dedicated to Eutychus, a popular charioteer of the day. There is a somewhat lighter touch in the prologue and also more confidence in the lasting quality of the poet's gift to literature. It is a long prologue and I will quote only a few lines which introduce a new idea about the fable.

Now briefly I will tell how fables came
To be invented. Once a helpless slave,
Because he dared not say the thing he would,
Transposed his feelings into fable form
And by fictitious jesting 'scaped the lash.
Now I have made a highway of his path,
Myself inventing more than he bequeathed,
At times to my own great calamity.

This third book has a wider scope than the first two, including anecdotes about Aesop and a long item on a contemporary subject. The epilogue has a touch of self-defense in the Horatian manner and is fairly outspoken in its claim on the patron's assistance. Book IV is addressed to an unknown Particulo, presumably an imperial freedman. Phaedrus by now shows real confidence. His fables are Aesopean rather than Aesop's and he scorns the illiterate mob who may not appreciate them. In the body of the book he speaks frequently in his own person and the epilogue is brief, pungent and self-satisfied.

There still are many things that I might tell
And plenty of variety therein.

> But cleverness is welcome when 'tis brief,
> Offensive if prolonged. So, my dear Sir,
> Particulo, whose name shall live through me
> As long as Latin letters keep their worth,
> If not my genius, praise my brevity
> The which more justly may commend the poet
> As poets can prove more pestilential pests.

The fifth book is a fragment but has a prologue without address which goes a step further in divorcing Phaedrus' work from that of Aesop.

> Whenever I make use of Aesop's name
> (To whom long since I've rendered what I owe)
> Tis done to borrow his authority,
> As certain artists do in these our times
> To enhance the value of their modern work:
> On their own sculpture write Praxiteles,
> Zeuxis on canvas, Myron on silver plate.
> So much does gnawing jealousy accord
> Antiquity above our triumphs new.

An Appendix consists of thirty fables no longer even remotely associated with Aesop, some of them of considerable length and amounting to short stories.

It is time to look at the verses themselves which compose Phaedrus' contribution to Latin literature. The simplest are the earliest, versified beast fables, usually with a moral attached either at the beginning or at the end, sometimes both. I.24 offers a typical example with the moral stated in advance.

> The helpless man who apes the strong is lost.
> Once on a time a frog beheld a bull
> Out in the field and, envying his size,
> Puffed out his wrinkled skin, then asked
> His brood of young: Am I as large as he?
> They answered, No. Again he puffed and swelled

And asked them which was larger, he or the bull.
The bull, said they. Then, in one mighty try,
He puffed and burst and lay, a ruptured corpse.

I.4 is of the same sort.

Rightly he'd lose his wealth who'd steal another's.
A dog with meat in mouth once swam a stream
And in the water saw his reflection clear.
Thinking to snatch a prize from the other dog,
He tried to seize it but, his greed deceived,
Both lost the morsel from his hungry jaw
And failed to grab the morsel which he sought.

In the first fable of all, the moral comes at the end.

Down to a river bank there came a wolf,
Likewise a lamb, both thirsty, wolf upstream
And far below, the lamb. From treacherous throat
The wolf in rage let out a quarrelsome snarl:
Why do you roil the water that I drink?
The lamb replied in terror: How, I pray,
Can I, sir Wolf, do what you say I do?
The water flows from you to where I drink.
Rebuffed by obvious truth, the wolf replied:
Six months ago you spoke a curse on me.
But no, the lamb said, I had not been born.
It was your father then, by Hercules.
And so he seized the lamb and swallowed him.
This tale is told for men we all know well
Who with false charges ruin the innocent.

Among the simpler fables we find our old friends, the fox and
the crow (I.13).

Who loves to hear men's specious flattery,
Too late repentant, shall pay heavy price.

Once when a crow had snatched a luscious cheese
From out a window and to devour it
Sat in a tree, a fox espied him there
And spake him thus: Oh crow, how radiant
Thy glossy wings, how glorious thy frame,
Noble thy countenance. Hadst thou a voice
No bird could equal thee. The stupid crow
To show his voice let fall the luscious cheese.
The crafty fox devoured it at a gulp.
And so too late the crow bewailed his fate.

Not so familiar to us is the fable of the foolish stag and his
antlers (I. 12).

This little tale is told to prove
That what you scorn may profit most.
A stag stood by a spring to drink
And in the water saw himself;
Astonished, praised his branching horns
But criticised his spindling legs.
Then, frightened by the huntsman's shout,
He fled light footed o'er the fields,
Escaped the dogs and reached the woods.
The trees entrapped his branching horns
Till he fell victim to the dogs.
Dying, they say, he spake these words:
Unhappy beast, at last I know
How useful what I chiefly scorned
And what I praised, what grief it brought.

One more quotation will be enough for these fables of the
simpler type. (I.11.)

The man who brags with naught to justify,
Though he fool strangers, makes his friends all laugh.
A lion with an ass would hunting go.
Clothing the ass with brush, he ordered him

To frighten with his bray the jungle beasts,
That he, the lion, might catch them as they fled.
So then the ass with all his might and main
Panicked the beasts with this strange miracle
And they in terror fled the forest paths
Only to be attacked by Leo's fangs,
Till, tired by slaughter, he addressed the ass:
Belay your braying. But the insolent beast
Answered: How think you was my vocal act?
Distinguished, said the lion; had I not known
Your character and race, I too had fled.

So much for the beast fable in its simplest form. It was not of sufficient general interest to satisfy an ambitious writer. Even in the first two books, if we are to believe the poet's claim, Phaedrus introduced enough mild political satire to get himself into some sort of trouble. It can hardly have been very serious, for only a few years later, Seneca had never heard of the fabulist. Phaedrus was following the technique of the young clerk Horace with his blatant and scurrilous early satires which sought at any cost the attention of the great. But Phaedrus was neither as courageous nor as able as young Horace and his attack on public attention is far less obvious and certainly less successful. The first touch of satire in the fables as we have them is aimed at the courts. (I.10).

Who once has gained the liar's name
No man believes when truth's his game.
Old Aesop's fable proves the same.
A wolf once called a fox a thief.
The fox, as guiltless, claimed relief.
An ape, the judge, assumed his place
And, after each had plead his case,
Thuswise distributed the blame:
You, wolf, did not lose what you claim
But you, sir fox, did steal the same.

More directly critical of the imperial regime is I.15.

When nations change their lords from time to time
The poor change nothing but their master's name.
That this is true my humble fable shows.
A timid ancient, pasturing his ass,
Was frightened by a sudden hostile shout.
He begged his ass to flee lest they be caught.
The ass, unhurried, questioned: Do you think
He'll put *two* packs upon me if he wins?
Why, no, the old man said. Then what care I
Who is my master while I bear my load?

Even under a strict censorship there could be little enough offence
in such verses as these, and it is of course possible that what we
have of Phaedrus is only a part, the uncensored part, of what he
originally published. But for me it is easier to believe that the in-
conspicuous Phaedrus was using conventional satiric means to
draw attention to himself, assuming an importance which he did
not have but hoped to win, and that, liking to think of himself as
a satirist, he took a certain pleasure in pretending that his verses
were really dangerous.

The characteristics of satire do appear increasingly through the
volume. Perhaps the first and simplest step in that direction lies in
the starting point of a fable, not from a general moral principal
proverbially stated but from some concrete and specific incident.
Fable I.6 deals with such an incident and although it deals with
animals it does not treat them in their relations with each other.
It is what we might well call an occasional poem dealing with a
specific incident and ending with a sharply made point.

The neighbors noted a thief's wedding day
And Aesop straightway had these words to say.
Once on a time the sun would take a wife
But all the frogs set up an unholy row,
Till Jupiter, disturbed by all their noise,
Inquired the cause. One denizen of the bog
Replied: Even now *one* sun dries up our swamp

And in the unwatered waste leaves us to die:
What will result if he beget a brood?

The distinction is not great but I think it has some significance. In the prologue to Book II Phaedrus states that Aesop furnishes "examples" for the moral benefit of mankind. To illustrate he attempts to give such an example but, with the candor and scepticism of the satirist, points out at the end its futility in face of human nature.

A lion lingered by a fallen steer.
Up comes a bandit and demands a share.
'Twere yours, he said, did you not always snatch,
And drove the bandit off. A traveller
By chance came innocently by the spot
But, seeing the lion, quietly withdrew.
But he, in kindly tones: Pray, have no fear;
Take freely what your modesty deserves.
Then carved the carcass into equal shares
And sought the woods, leaving the man to choose.
An excellent fable worthy of your praise;
But greed's still rich and modesty's still poor.

The very brief fable which opens Book III deals with a specific incident, presents no animals at all and, at the end, suggests a hidden implication, presumably political.

Once an old woman saw an empty jar
Still redolent of good Falernian wine,
Spreading delightful odor on the breeze.
The greedy dame with eager nostrils smelled
And cried: Oh, blessed soul, what shall I say
Thou wert when thy remains are still so sweet?
What this tale means he'll tell who knows my mind.

Another non-animal fable (III.9) has the satiric touch and also foreshadows the type of epigram which Martial was to establish, the epigram with the surprise punch at the end.

The name of friend is common, friendship rare.
When Socrates had built his little house
(Whose death I would not fear to win his fame;
Envy I'd bear if death gave recompense.)
Some joker from the crowd was heard to say:
Why, pray, so great a man, so small a house?
Said he: Would I could fill it with *true* friends.

It would seem that Phaedrus, having had some success with his first two books, was ambitious to expand his medium. The first step was to introduce into the third and following books more fables which did not deal with animals but with people. The second step was to introduce longer anecdotes but still with a moral expressly pointed out either at the beginning or at the end. Finally he dropped the moral and in the Appendix there appeared "*fabulae*" or "*fabellae*" which were out and out short stories or anecdotes. "The Widow of Ephesus" (Appendix, 13) is a good example. There is still the suggestion of a moral in the satiric last line.

A wife once lost her husband whom she loved
And had long since consigned him to the tomb
While none could lure her from the sepulcher
Where she still poured her shattered life in tears.
Her fame for chaste devotion spread apace.
Meanwhile some bandits who had robbed Jove's shrine
Were crucified to satisfy the god.
And, that no man should take their bodies down
For burial, strong guards were given post
Hard by the tomb wherein the widow wept.
It happened that a soldier from the guard,
Thirsty one night begged water from the maid
Who sat there by the widow as she slept,
Having watched long beside her husband's corpse.
So, through the open door, the soldier saw
The widow, pale yet beauteous to behold.

At once his heart was seized with sudden fire
Till soon he burned with lust beyond control.
A clever chap, he found renewed excuse
To see the widow time and time again
Till, softened by their daily intercourse,
She came by stages to endure the man
And presently to feel a warmer bond.
So, while the guard spent all his nights with her,
One of the bodies of the crucified
Was stolen, to the terror of the guard.
He told the widow. She said: Have no fear,
And gave her husband's body for the cross
That so her lover might not suffer harm.
So shame usurped the fair abode of praise.

Appendix 14 is another example of the short story, a story with no apparent moral but again ending with a suspiciously ironic last line.

Two youthful lovers wooed a single maid.
One, rich, o'ermatched the poor man's looks and name.
The appointed wedding day arrived at last.
The losing lover bearing ill his grief
Betook him to his little garden plot
Near where the groom's fine villa would receive
The maiden from her mother's loving arms.
(The house in town was scorned as far too small.)
The feast is spread, the crowding guests arrive
And Hymenaeus waves the wedding torch.
The poor man's little ass that served his trade
Was standing idle by the city gate.
So him the parents by chance impressed to spare
Their daughter's delicate feet the stony trip.
By Venus' grace the heavens in sudden storm
Were shattered, thunder filled the universe,
Spreading dark night buried in dreadful cloud.
The light was gone and straightway hurtling hail

Had scattered all the host of wedding guests.
Each sought in headlong flight some safe retreat.
The little ass turned to his well known home
And with loud voice made known his presence there.
The slaves run up, behold the maiden fair
With wondering gaze—then bear the master word.
He lay at table with his special friends
Drowning his love with many a brimming cup.
His heart relieved, he heard the servants' cries.
With Bacchus urging him and Venus too,
He straight performed a wedding of his own.
The parents sought the maid, the heralds cried,
The one-time groom bewailed his vanished bride.
The town soon learned the course events had taken
And all men praised the ways of providence.

The more Phaedrus wrote the more confidence he acquired in his own powers as a writer. He seems to have conceived the desire to be more than a fabulist, to be a satirist. But he never had or acquired a sense of artistic form and his point of view was always a somewhat superficial one. He made a short step toward the development of the satiric epigram and this won for him the only recognition which antiquity granted him. For Martial spoke of him once though not too favorably. In one of his epigrams (III.20) he mentions "the trifles of naughty Phaedrus." Perhaps it would be well to leave it at that. But one more item must be added to Phaedrus' modest credit. As he lengthened his poems he did instinctively introduce such bits of color as the storm at the wedding and the changing emotions of "The Widow of Ephesus". His urbanity increased and his irony gained point. It is hardly fair to compare Phaedrus with the master of Latin Satire, but Horace's use of the fable in his Satire on the joys of his Sabine farm shows vividly the difference between the simple telling of a fable and the artistic use of the fable as illustrative material in a Satire. In speaking of his leisurely conversations with his country neighbors of a wintry evening, Horace says:

Then Cervius very likely will produce
Some old wife's tale to embroider well his point.
There may be envious praise of weary wealth
That haunts Arellius. Cervius takes his cue:
Once on a time, says he, a country mouse,
Tradition has it, in his meager hole
Was entertaining for old friendship's sake
A city mouse. Close fisted and perforce
Guarding his savings, still he could relax
In hospitality. Forth from his hoard
He brought, unsparing, cherished bits of corn,
A few hard peas and fragments half consumed
Of bacon rind, seeking to overcome
The jaded appetite of his city guest
That with fastidious tooth suspiciously
Touched each new offering, while the country host
Stretched on a thorny couch of new-cut chaff,
Ate spelt and darnel uncomplainingly.
Finally in despair the city mouse
Burst forth: "My friend, how can you bear to live
Forever in this god-forsaken hole?
Won't you set forth with me and learn to know
Cities and men rather than these wild wastes?
Take to the road nor let yourself forget
That we who tread the earth have mortal souls:
Nor great nor small can miss the call of death.
Live while you can, get pleasure nor forget
That life is short." This urbane argument
Persuaded in a trice the country mouse.
Out of his hole he sprang. The two set forth
Eager to reach the city walls by dark.
Already Night had traversed half its course
When they two crept into the wealthy house
Where ivory couches stood with coverlets
Of Tyrian purple, and upon the board
Heaping remains of yester evening's feast.

The city mouse, turned host, bade his rude guest
Recline upon the couch. Gaily himself
He played the part of slave, dispensing food
And dainties, stealing a taste of each before
Serving his rustic friend who well content,
Lolled there in pleasure at his changed estate.
Sudden, the mighty din of opening doors
Drove host and guest from off the banquet couch.
Hither and yon they rushed while rising howls
Of watch dogs added to their frenzied fright.
Then spake the country mouse: "No life for me
Is this. Farewell; my simple country hole
Will comfort me with safety and plain fare."

The contrast with Phaedrus' method of telling a story is obvious at once. Such moral as the fabulist has to point is baldly stated in lines outside the story proper. He does not create a background and atmosphere nor develop suggestively the parallelism between man and animal. He has no dramatic build-up or artistic contrast. He tells a plain tale simply and concisely. And this is as it should be. Phaedrus may have cherished vague hopes of becoming a Satirist, yet it is not as such that he will be remembered but rather as the forthright teller of simple tales and the purveyor of beast fables with their peculiar appeal to every age of human history.

CHAPTER THREE

Manilius

PHAEDRUS SET FOR himself a modest goal. His contemporary Manilius, in sharp contrast, undertook to expound in hexameter verse the astrology of Stoicism as Lucretius had presented the atomism of Epicurus. His prologue, however, shows a purpose rather more akin to that of Horace than to that of Lucretius. Manilius is conscious of doing something *new* in the field of *poetry*. He is interested more in adding another element to Rome's conquest of Greek poetic literature than in helping mankind. His opening word, *carmine*, is repeated like a refrain throughout his long introduction, and although he rightly claims a twofold interest, *carminis et rerum,* he emphasizes most the fact that he is the first to rouse Helicon with these new songs. His is an *opus non ullis ante sacratum carminibus.*

Nothing whatever is known of the life of M. Manilius, the author of the *Astronomica.* A reference to the defeat of Varus (I. 899) places the beginning of his work at least as late as 9 A.D. The term *pater patriae* applied to the emperor (I.925) must refer to Augustus rather than to Tiberius, who never accepted the title. But the reference to Rhodes (IV.764) as the retreat of him who was to rule Rome could hardly have been written before Tiberius was confirmed as the successor of Augustus. It is therefore fairly certain that the *Astronomica* was begun after 9 A.D. and that the later books were written after 14 A.D. The work is still incomplete when it breaks off abruptly in Book IV.

In spite of its title, Manilius' poem is really concerned with astrology rather than astronomy. The first book prepares the way. After a prologue of 117 lines Manilius devotes another 128 lines to the origin of the world, its place in the universe and its spherical form. Various theories of creation are discussed and no single one affirmed. Nevertheless,

> This grand creation of the universe
> Corporeal, with Nature's many parts
> Composed of air and fire, of earth and sea,
> Is ruled by superhuman wisdom. God
> Breathes on his world and governs silently,
> With Reason's might dispensing faithfully
> To each component part its rightful share.

The rest of Book I is largely descriptive astronomy covering the signs of the zodiac and the stars and winding up with comets and meteors. The other three books develop the art of astrology, the effect of the signs of the zodiac on mankind and on the earth and the whole process of interpreting the decrees of Fate by an understanding of the intimations which Fate gives through the constellations of the sky.

There can be no doubt of the earnestness of Manilius in combatting Epicureanism and in presenting the arguments for a controlled universe. His mastery of the science of astrology was probably no more complete than his presentation of it, and the *Astronomica* is no more a handbook of astrology than Vergil's *Georgics* are a practical guide to the farmer. Lucretius fell short of the experts in the materialistic science of his day. But both Vergil and Lucretius left poems which have held their place among the world's classics not because of what they added to man's scientific knowledge but because of their understanding of the pity in the world and their appeal to man's humanity. Manilius, writing in and for a world already drastically changed, lacked the human appeal for which the new rhetoric could offer no adequate substitute. And yet it is as a poet that Manilius presents himself and as a poet he has some importance for the understanding of the transition from Augustan to Silver Latin literature.

My song invokes from heaven the plan divine
Hid in the stars, conspirators with Fate,
The stars that rule the fluctuating course
Of human life. By heavenly Reason taught,
I shall be first to waken Helicon
With this new music, stirring with new life
The swaying treetops on her summit green,
Bringing from far offerings no poet has brought
Before. Thou, Caesar, dost inspire who art
Both prince and father of thy country. Thou
That swayest with august law the obedient world
To win that heaven bestowed upon thy sire.
From thee comes strength to venture that vast song.
The universe relaxed in such vast peace
Favors my enterprise and would itself
Concede the heavenly secrets to my verse.
I would fare forth through ether's realm to live
At large in spacious heaven and learn to know
The constellations and the contrary paths
Of all the stars. Yet not enough were this.
I'd know the deepest purpose that resides
Within the mighty universe, the way
Whereby with signs it rules, ay, first begets
All living things. Then would I set the whole
To ordered music, Phoebus for my guide.
Two altars shine for me with stablished flame;
I pray before two shrines with passions twain:
Music and Matter.

This statement of purpose by Manilius is important for at least two characteristics, the elaboration of his objectives, information and poetry, and the dedication to Augustus. In the first place there is definite reminiscence of former poets. The key word, *carmen* used three times, once in the first line, once in the middle and once in the last line, recalls Horace's claim, *carmina non prius audita Musarum sacerdos canto.* But Vergil too had begun both of his major works with the verb *cano* and, in the *Georgics,* he calls on Apollo for help. Lucretius wrote:

> With mind alerted I am traversing
> The pathless regions of the Pierides
> Untrodden else by any foot of man.

It is not a question of imitation: the important thing is that Manilius considered himself, like Lucretius and Horace and Vergil (yes, and like the lesser Phaedrus) a pioneer in a new field of poetry. The dedication to Augustus is slightly different. Vergil had offered his tribute to Augustus in an indirect fashion in the prophecy of Book VI of the *Aeneid.* Horace had written odes to Augustus. Lucretius had addressed his poem in somewhat fulsome terms to Memmius as Manilius does to Augustus. There is no indication that Augustus was a patron of the poet or that he had suggested the writing of the poem. Nor is the address extravagant. Nevertheless, the very fact of addressing the emperor directly and the touch of flattery, slight as it may seem, indicates the first step toward the wild extravagance of some of the later imperial poets. It is significant that in the three other didactic poems which have survived from approximately the same time we find striking similarities of prologue ideas. Grattius, in his treatise on hunting, is not really significant but he begins with *dona divum cano* and emphasizes *carmen* at the close of his introduction. Germanicus, in his "translation" of Aratus, also insists that he is a poet, that what he writes is a *carmen,* and he pleads with Tiberius as Lucretius did with Venus and Manilius with Augustus for the maintenance of peace in order that poetry may have a chance. The writer of the anonymous *Aetna* begins abruptly with *carmen erit,* calls on Apollo for help and insists on the novelty of his subject. There is not much of importance here, simply the traces of that change from the concise statement of subject and simple dedication which characterised the Augustan poets to the extravagance of a Lucan or a Statius.

No one would doubt for a moment that a poet undertaking to expound Stoic doctrine in hexameter verse was emulating Lucretius and attempting to refute his thesis. This is of course just what

Manilius was doing. If the fact needed confirmation it would be found in I.486. With considerable eloquence he is arguing the effective reason of god as against the chance meeting of atoms and he uses the splendid words so familiar from Lucretius, *moenia mundi*. The remarkable thing, however, is that, after many sustained efforts, no scholar has been able to produce more than a few echoes of the earlier poet and these not wholly convincing. He bears out his own claim made in II.57ff.

> I'll sing my own song—to no other poet
> Will I be debtor for my verses. Theft
> Is not my aim but work of my own mind.
> In chariot unique I'll soar to heaven
> And in my own ship sail the sea: I'll sing
> Of Nature's placid god all-powerful
> Who permeates the heaven, the earth, the sea.

An orthodox Stoicism pervades the whole poem and emerges in more than one familiar commonplace. The prologue contains this statement of the development of civilisation: (I.75–90.)

> Gold still lay hidden in the lonely hills,
> Uncharted seas concealed new continents.
> Man dared not trust himself to Ocean's realm,
> His hopes to stormy winds and each knew well
> It was enough to know himself. But when
> Long days had sharpened his intelligence
> And toil had mothered wit in wretched man,
> When Fortune with hard lessons taught mankind
> To fend for its own weal, then men explored
> In all directions. What experience,
> Wise teacher, showed, they shared to common good.
> Twas then the barbarous tongue received the laws,
> The wandering sailor penetrated then
> The ocean blind and trade opened the way
> To unknown lands. And so antiquity
> Revealed the arts of peace and war, for ever
> Experience sows the seeds of something new.

At times the tone approaches that of Satire with its attacks on wealth and foolish desires but on the whole the passages which digress from the strictly astrological are of a more serious Stoic character with comparatively little intrusion of Satiric allusion. Two selections from the fourth book (1 ff. and 387 ff.) have a familiar ring of satire:

> Why do we waste a life of worried years
> Tortured by fears and deep desire for wealth?
> Old from eternal care, we seek long life
> But lose it and with never a blessed hour
> From answered prayer, we play the part of men
> Who'll live forever—but we never live.
> Each man is poorer as he prays for more
> Nor ever counts the things he has, but hopes
> For what he has not. While our nature asks
> For little, we with prayer accumulate
> Makings of mighty ruin and we buy
> Luxury with our gains, with luxury
> Buy poverty. The highest bid for wealth
> Is waste of wealth. Come, mortals that you are,
> Relax your souls, spare life its woeful plaints,
> Fate rules the world, fixed laws rule everything:
> All time is marked by ordered flux. Our death
> Is fixed at birth, our end stems from its source.

*****

> "A mighty effort, ay, and intricate
> You would demand and once again you plunge
> My mind in darkness when I seemed to see
> The light by feeble reasoning exposed."
> Your goal is god, your aim to scale the heavens
> And, born by law of Fate, to learn the fates.
> The goal is worth the toil, but such reward
> Is not without its price. So marvel not
> At windings in the way and fastnesses.
> Enough that we may enter: all the rest

Is ours to master. If the tempting gold
Remain not undiscovered and earth retain
Her treasure buried you will traverse earth
To gather jewels, yea and scour the seas
For wealth: the careworn peasant anxiously
Will pray for profit only; then, alas,
How vastly shall his fields deceive his hopes!
Wealth only will become our goal pursued
With trading ships or armies, booty-mad.
Shame on us so to worship transient wealth!
War feeds on luxury, the stomach gloats
On plunder and your heir sighs for your death.
What shall we then begrudge to win to god?
The whole man must be spent that god may dwell
Within him.

The first of these two selections comes from the prologue to Book IV. Each book begins with introductory verses whose purpose seems to be primarily to break the monotony of the technical material and to substantiate Manilius' claim to be equally interested in science and poetry. The second book opens with a eulogy of Homer and Hesiod, passing on to the productions of poets who have been in one way or another predecessors in his own field. Book III makes almost a new start: the poet is about to penetrate new fields and makes a new invocation to the Muses. He lists the more popular fields of epic and renounces them in favor of new subject matter, a very definite appeal to the interest of his audience.

Now as I soar to higher realms and dare
Extend my power nor fear to penetrate
Regions unvisited, be ye my guides,
Ye Muses. For I seek to expand your realm
And add new worthy measures to my song.
I shall not sing of wars to wreck high heaven
Nor mothers with their offspring seared by flames
Of lightning, nor conspiracies of kings,

Nor, with the fall of Troy, Hector redeemed
By Priam. I'll not sing the Colchian maid
Selling her father's kingdom . . .

*****

The first beginning of the Roman race,
The city's great, alternate war and peace,
Till all the world bowed to one people's laws—
All this must wait. Tis easy to spread sail
Before the favoring breeze, by various arts
To cultivate a fertile plot, add gold
And ivory to adorn a surface fair
By its own nature. Far too tame the task,
Too simply done, to fashion verse replete
With scintillating tales. My task to tell
In meter things unknown by name, the times
And seasons of the changing universe.

It is not only in the prologues that Manilius seeks to win and hold the interest of his audience. It is true that the historical excursus used in Book IV to prove the rule of Fate follows directly on the Stoic appeal already noted and is part of the introduction to the book; also that it is one of the longest digressions. But even more striking is the excursus in Book I (758–804) which illustrates at considerable length the theory held by some that the Milky Way consists of the souls of heroes. This gives the poet opportunity to fill his page with famous names and especially to introduce his roll of honor of Roman heroes culminating with Augustus. As though this were insufficient relief, a second similar digression follows shortly (874–926) which the poet introduces to show the influence of comets, the plague at Athens and the wars of Rome both foreign and civil.

The most illuminating digression is the story of Perseus and Andromeda in Book V. It must be read in its entirety to appreciate the tendencies which it illustrates.

Next constellation is Andromeda
Which, Pisces being risen, proceeds all bright
Within the twelfth arc of the northern sky.
This maiden once her parents' dreadful guilt
Betrayed to torture when the hostile sea
With all its might beset them. Storm-wrecked earth
Was soon submerged and what was once their realm
Became the sea. One price to save their fate
Was named: to offer to the raging sea
Andromeda, that so a monstrous beast
Might feast upon her gentle limbs. This was
Her hymeneal rite, her progeny
The assuaging of the public loss. She wept
As they adorned their victim with the robe
For other rites prepared. The living maid
Was hurried to a funeral void of death.

So when they reached at last the cruel shore
Her delicate arms were stretched on the rough cliff,
Her ankles fastened to the rock with chains.
So on her virgin cross the maiden hung
To wait for death. Yet in her dire distress
Her proud poise failed not nor her modesty:
Seemly her pleading and her snow white neck
Bowed modestly, her shield her purity,
As from her shoulders slipped her mantle's folds,
The tunic from her arms, and all about
Her shoulders fell her long dishevelled locks.

Around thee halcyons fluttering their wings
Bewailed thy fate in mournful harmony
And made for thee cool shade with pinions joined.
At sight of thee the ocean checked its waves
Nor pounded with its wonted force the shore.
A Nereid, rising from the salty deep,

In pity mourned thy fortune and thy youth.
The very breeze with gentle breath refreshed
Thy hanging limbs and caroled mournfully.
By happy chance, that day brought Perseus back
Victor at last over the Gorgon curse.
Seeing the maiden hanging on the cliff,
His face went rigid which no enemy
Had so disturbed: his hand but barely held
His trophy and Medusa's conqueror
Was conquered by Andromeda. Straightway
His jealousy leaped up against the cliff.
Happy, he cried, the chains that hold those limbs.
And when from her he learned the reason why
She hung there, straight he swore to wade
Through war to Ocean's wedding couch, his wrath
Quenching his terror lest new gorgons come.

He soars aloft, with promises of life
Revives the weeping parents, wins from them
A marriage compact, speeds back to the shore.
But now the sea was roused. In serried ranks
The breakers fled before a mighty beast
That broke the waters with its head and belched
Forth brine. The sea echoed its gnashing teeth.
Head on it sails, threatening with mighty horn,
Crowding the ocean. Phocys fills all space
With din. The mountains tremble and the cliff.

Unhappy maid, despite thy champion!
What then had been thy mien? What breezes bore
Thy spirit forth? When every drop of blood
Had fled thy limbs and from the crannied cliff
Thine eyes beheld the advancing enemy?
How small a victim for so vast a sea.

Then on his spread wings, Perseus, poised in heaven,
Hurled with unerring aim the shaft he'd dipped

In Gorgon blood and struck the enemy.
It reared against its foe and, changing front,
Rose glittering with its scales, its whole expanse
Lifting to strike. But Perseus, as it rose
From out the deep, withdrew in unison
Through yielding air, eluded the attack
And struck the attacking front. The dreadful beast
Quailed not before the hero but in rage
Snarled at the breeze and gnashed its teeth in vain,
Blowing the brine to heaven and drenching so
The flying warrior with the bloody stream
And sprinkling all the stars. The maiden, cause
Of battle, watched the battle's course until
Forgetful of herself she feared for him,
Her champion, breathing hard, suspended now
In mind as well as body. At long last
The monster sank back to the water's face
With many a deadly wound and swam again
The ocean's surface, yet to the maiden still
Too terrifying for her to behold.
Perseus, within the ocean's calmer depths,
Washed clean his body, mightier than before,
And soared triumphant to the lofty cliff.
There he released the maiden from her chains,
His war-won bride, pledged by his victory.

In the first place, the story is not artistically incorporated into the narrative. The transitions are abrupt, even awkward, leaving the distinct impression of a purple patch deliberately inserted. In reading the tale it is impossible not to think of the Aristaeus myth used by Vergil in the *Georgics* and the Ariadne story in Catullus' epyllion. In one the hero overpowers a sea god and in the other a deserted heroine is rescued. The Aristaeus myth is disproportionately long but it is introduced naturally and the Ariadne story is the heart of the epyllion. Manilius must have had Catullus' tale in mind for he borrows the conceit *funera nec funera* (Cat. 64.83) to make his own *sine funere funus* (1.549) and, except as a reminiscence of Ariadne's draperies washing about at her feet, it is hard to accept Andromeda's unnecessary nudity which serves only as the motive for rhetorical detail. The important matter is, however, that the whole story is told with considerable rhetorical effect and an atmosphere of melodramatic horror but without a touch of real human feeling. If there had been any such warmth it would have been dissipated when the hero leaves beauty in distress and goes off to draw up a wedding contract with her grieving parents. There is an unreality throughout, a feeling produced by a combination of the technique of the artificial love elegy and that of the rhetorical drama and epic that was to come in the time of Nero. There is none of the passion of Catullus or the pity of Vergil, none of the true poetry of either. There are numerous epigrammatic phrases and lines such as *spectabat pugnam pugnandi causa puella.* But rhetoric cannot compensate for a lack of humanity.

Manilius was convinced that he was making an original contribution to Rome's conquest of the field of poetry, but he came too late to profit by the Augustan atmosphere of creative enthusiasm and lacked the inspired humanity of Vergil or Lucretius. He wrote an adequate verse treatise on astrology but he did not have the poet's passion that would justify a scientist in abandoning prose.

CHAPTER FOUR

Persius

THE MEMOIRS OF SENECA the Elder have preserved the cold facts about the recitation mania which was almost co-eval with the Christian era. The first Satire of Persius breathes life into these facts. It also adds its convincing evidence to what has been suggested, that a great spate of poetry or, perhaps better, verse, of the Julio-Claudian age has been lost. While Persius stands apart, in his own estimation, from his fellow poets, assailing them with evident sincerity, nevertheless he exhibits well their most striking characteristics.

Aulus Persius Flaccus was born at Volaterrae in 34 A.D. into an environment of some wealth and considerable social standing. He was connected with the family of Arria, wife of Paetus Thrasea, the stubborn Stoic and victim of Nero. Persius lost his father at the age of six and when he was twelve was sent to Rome where his two masters were successively Remmius Palaemon, grammarian, and Verginius Flavus, rhetorician. The former was notorious for his low character albeit the most popular teacher of the day. It seems possible that Persius' aversion to immorality was due rather more to the revulsion of a candid nature from the well-known irregularities of his first teacher than to the earlier secluded years of life under the care of female relatives. The traditional picture of Persius as a shielded product of feminine possessiveness living the secluded life of a scholar in a library cannot stand up against the facts of his early years. What did affect his whole outlook on life in his early twenties was certainly his practical adoption, at perhaps sixteen or seventeen, by the Stoic philosopher, Cornutus, under whom he was a fellow-pupil of Lucan. His own words are the best evidence of this. (V. 30–40.)

When first the crimson garb of childhood
Ceased to protect me and my birthday charm
Was hung as offering to the household gods,
When friends became intriguing and the folds
Of a white toga sent my wandering eye
O'er the Subura without shame or pain,
Just when the path of life breeds troublous doubt
And ignorant error leads the bewildered mind
Toward branching cross-roads, then it was I gave
Myself into your hands, youth that I was.
You took me straight, Cornutus to your heart
Socratic. Then, with neatly hidden guile,
Your rule made straight my twists of character
Until my mind, subdued by reason, strove
To be controlled and, neath your sculptor's thumb,
Take on new features.

The young Persius, then, trained in rhetoric by Verginius Rufus
(author of a treatise highly commended by Quintilian and granted
high distinction by Tacitus) and afterwards dominated by a distinguished Stoic philosopher, began writing before the two great
influences of his education had had time to fuse. As a result, what
he wrote was often very difficult to understand. Too much matter, insufficiently analysed, pours forth in confusion. There is
often inconsistency and rarely complete clarity. The urge to be
startling and so to command attention conflicts with the desire to
expound a doctrine and to convince. At the moment our concern
is with the rhetorical characteristics and they emerge all too vividly
in the first Satire. (I.1-12.)

"Alas for human worries! What a void
There is in nature!" "Who will read that stuff?"
"You're asking me? No one, by Hercules."
"No one?" "Well, one or two—or none." "How mean
And shameful." "Why? Because you fear, perhaps,
That Polydamas and the Trojan dames

Will find their Labeo better? Nonsense, friend.
If crazy Rome makes light of aught, *you* won't
Step up and rectify the lying scales
Nor look outside yourself to prove your case.
For who at Rome has not—ah, could I speak.
And yet why not when I see these gray hairs
And all the grimness of the life we lead
When once we leave behind our childhood toys
And smack of uncles? Give me leave." "I won't."
"What shall I do then? Mine's a mean guffaw."

Horace had begun his first satire with the calm and rational words, "How comes it, Maecenas, that no man lives content with the life which reason or chance has given him?" That Persius took Horace as his literary progenitor is hardly open to question but how different his approach. He demands attention and yet he does not make his thesis clear. Horace leads his reader gently and persuasively; Persius shocks his listener into attention and bewilders him. The hypothetical opponent was a device well-developed by Horace but he always made the situation clear by such a phrase as "someone may say" or else he carefully set the stage for a realistic dialogue. Persius assumes the use of spoken tone and inflection to convey the information that there *is* an interlocutor. Then he angles for the hearer's interest by a composite reference to Lucilius and Lucretius and an allusion to Homer just learned enough to intrigue and flatter a not too brilliant audience. This audience is still in mind when he breaks off what promises to be a daring insult to the populace of Rome, leaving them in tantalizing expectation and winding up his introductory paragraph with a word (*cachino*, guffaw) either from the vernacular slang or coined by himself.

With the introduction out of the way—without too much illumination proffered as to what the real subject is to be—Persius proceeds to attack the current crop of writers through their vehicle of publication. Here is his picture of the public recitation. (I.13–30.)

We sit at home and write, some verse, some prose,
All grandiose for lungs of bounteous breath
To bellow forth. This for the public show
When nicely combed and in your toga new,
Wearing your birthday ring, all decked in white,
You'll read from that high platform, rinsing well
With modulating scales your agile throat,
Rolling a wanton eye. Whereat you'll see
Our burly sons of ancient Roman stock
In shameless movement and distracted voice
Shake with emotion when, the enticing song
Possessing every nerve, their inmost parts
Are tickled by the rhythm of the verse.
Will you cull tidbits for another's ears,
Old gray-beard, till you're forced to cry, Enough?
"What end for learning without some such yeast—
If the wild fig tree in you can't emerge?"
"Behold the scholar's pallor, his ripe growth!
Alas for our good name! Is it no use
For you to know if no one knows you know?"
"But it is fine to have men point you out,
Saying, That's he. Have you no wish to be
The school-book of a hundred curly kids?"

Exaggerated, of course. But Persius has hit upon the most essential weakness of this post-Augustan poetry: it is imitative, artificial, pretentious. It is so because the poet does not seek to express what may satisfy his own soul or the competent critic of the
future but only to satisfy his own vanity and win the applause of
an audience wholly unqualified to criticise. The audience too
shares the blame. They are the chief target in the lines which follow, depicting a banquet at which, for entertainment, an "artist"
reads the verses of some recently deceased poet. (I. 31–43.)

See where they lie, the sons of Romulus,
Well fed, among their cups, and call for news
Of the great world of poetry. Whereupon
One with a hyacinthine cloak about

His shoulders rants, with snivelling smirk, some trash
In drivelling verse, Phyllis or Hipsypile,
Or any mawkish product of the poets,
His filtered words balanced in delicate tones.
The heroes all applaud. So are not now
The ashes of the poet more blessed? Does not
The stone rest now more lightly on his bones?
The lesser guests praise too. Shall there not spring
From his remains, the ashes in his tomb,
A burst of violets? "You mock," he says,
"Indulge too much your scornful nostrils. Say,
Can any willingly refuse to win
Popular praise or give posterity
Verse that rates cedar oil, not fish or herbs?"

The poet is less obscure as he approaches what would seem to be the heart of his essay. (To his readers, the use of cedar oil to preserve good books and the use of worthless books as waste paper to wrap up market products for delivery would be wholly familiar.) He makes it clear that what has gone before has been preparatory by a more formal recognition of his hypothetical adversary and by direct expression of his own position. (I.44–62.)

"Whoe'er you are whom I have made my foe
I'm not the man, if I have written aught
That's passing good—a rare bird, you'll admit—
But if I have, I'm not one, I'll confess,
To fear men's praise: My heart is not of horn.
But I insist the ultimate goal is not
Your "Bravo", "Splendid." Just shake out those terms:
What do they not contain? Is there not there
Attius' Iliad, drunk with hellebore?
Will you not find the little elegies
Produced by our elite before their feast
Is well digested? Everything that's spawned
On citron couches? You expertly serve
Your guests a hot sow's paunch; you gracefully

Give to your shivering friend a worn out cloak.
And then you say: I love the truth; speak out
The truth about myself. How can they so?
But, if you will, *I'll* say: You old bald pate,
You're just a trifler, you with that great mass
Ventricular, protruding half a yard.
Oh, lucky Janus: no stork's pecking bill
Clacks at your rear nor hand that imitates
The donkey's ear nor tongue down hanging like
A thirsty hound's in hot Apulia.
But you, my friends patrician, with no eyes
Behind, turn round and face the rear guard gibes.

There would probably be no insuperable difficulties here for a contemporary of the poet's if he had time to give it some thought. The citron wood couch, a collector's item, winds up one phase of the argument, that the praise of the guests is indiscriminate. The transition to the second phase, that the praise is calculated and cannot be sincere, is abrupt and deliberately rough, to be contrasted presently with the smooth joint which the fingernail cannot detect. Also Persius, fascinated by his own conceit of the double-faced Janus, carries too far the accompanying picture of small boys' contemptuous gestures. The interlocutor gets him back to the direct line of argument. (I.63–68.)

"What is the public's verdict?" What, indeed.
Save that at last our verses smoothly roll,
So smooth the nail can scarce detect the joints.
The poet can rule a verse as though he drew
A mason's line, squinting with one eye closed.
Or, if his job's to paint our character
To assail our luxury, our bourgeois feasts,
The Muse inspires still the grandiose.

Everything which is written to-day, Persius proceeds to claim, is on the flamboyant side, grandiose and pompous, resorting even to archaisms for striking effect. (I.69–82.)

Behold, what great heroic sentiments
We see produced by men whose wont has been
To trifle in Greek verse, picturing now
Some grove or now singing of country life
Complete with baskets, hearth fires, pigs and all
The smoking hay of Pales' holiday.
Whence there emerges Remus and yourself,
Old Quintius, wearing your plowshare bright
In furrows deep until your frantic wife
Clothes you Dictator where the cattle stand
And lictors bring the plow home. Bravo, Poet!

Now, here's a man dotes on the stringy book
Of drunken Accius. Some there are who love
Pacuvius and his foul Antiope
Whose dolorous heart survives on miseries.
Such is the fodder which our blear-eyed sires
Feed to their boys and can you therefore ask
Whence comes the hotch-potch in our style to-day,
Whence the abysmal taste which titillates
Our smooth shorn cavaliers along the aisles?

The poet digresses at this point to show that forensic oratory
has gone equally astray but the interlocutor recalls him to poetry
and quotes sample lines of the new products at which Persius
scoffs. He finally decides that, since he finds no sympathetic hearing, he will bury the jest which he tried to make at the beginning
of the Satire and so preserve it for his own satisfaction: "Who is
there who has not a donkey's ears?" Then, to end the whole discussion, he answers, a bit obliquely, the question which he posed
in the second line of the Satire, who will read stuff like that?
(I.123–134.)

Whoe'er you are that reads Cratinus still
For inspiration or grows pale from long
Perusal of the angry Eupolis
And too the grand old man of Comedy,

Look here as well and you may find perchance
Something well seasoned. Come then if you will
With ears prepared by these and you'll not find
The cheap guffaws at slippers of the Greeks
Or someone calling names in arrogant
Conceit because, supine in rustic pride,
He once as aedile smashed at Arretium
The short pint measures. No, nor him who laughs
At diagrams in sand and bursts with joy
When some pert harlot pulls a wise man's beard.
For such, the daily news and, after lunch,
Callirhoe.

It is perhaps significant that no one has been able to give a convincing explanation of the last word.

In conjunction with this first Satire should be considered fourteen lines of choliambic verse which have survived in the manuscripts and which may have been intended as a prologue to the volume. They present, in an involved and symbolic manner, the purpose of the poet.

I never drenched my lips in the Nag's spring;
I don't remember dreaming on two-peaked
Parnassus, to wake up a full blown poet;
The maids of Helicon, Pirene pale
I leave to those about whose images
The ivy clings. Myself, as yet but half
Initiate, I bring my humble verse
To the poet's festival. Who was it taught
The parrot his 'good day', the magpie too
To imitate our words so patiently?
It was the belly, master of art, the goad
Of wit, devising speech 'gainst Nature's law.
So, if there flash some hope of devious wealth
You'd think the poet crow, the poetess pie,
Were singing forth pure draughts of Pegasus.

Quite obviously, the suggested motive for writing, the necessity of earning a living, is frivolous. Persius was independently wealthy. What the lines really indicate is a self-conscious writer, young and unknown as a poet, (*semi-paganus* certainly means "half in the clan" rather than "half a country bumpkin") seeking to ingratiate himself with his hearers. First, in imitation of Horace, he renounces elevated or inspired poetry, presumably epic poetry, for it was Ennius who drank of Hippocrene and dreamed on Parnassus. Second, neither here nor in the first Satire does Persius address a patron or one to whom the Satires are dedicated. He brings his verse to the *sacra vatum*, the festival of poets, the rites of the clan of which he is on the waiting list. If, as a neophyte, he were addressing the Scipionic Circle or that of Maecenas, he would be likely to reserve his witty slang for a better occasion. He speaks with a deliberate frivolity designed to trap attention. It is hard not to believe that this attention was that of a group of "poets and critics" gathered at a social affair.

Beneath the assumed informality of the lines there is a suggestion of formal construction in the prologue. The nag of line one turns up as Pegasus in the last line and the draughts from his spring appear in both first and last lines. The skit is divided equally between the personal, direct presentation in the first half and the more symbolic appeal in the second. The symmetrical form so much favored by the neoterics has become commonplace.

To revert to style, there is much the same statement of principle in Satire V, lines 1–29.

"The poets all plead a hundred voices' aid,
A hundred mouths, a hundred tongues to sing,
Whether they plan to write grim tragedy
Or tell the Parthian's wounds who draws the shaft
From shattered groin." "What are you driving at?
What are these mighty gobbets of crude song?
You'd ply us with, to need a hundred throats?
Let those who'd sing in mightier strain collect
The mists of Helicon, who boil again

The pots of Procne and Thyestes, so to feed
The stupid Glyco. You're not squeezing air
In windy bellows till the metal glows
Within the furnace nor, in smothered tones,
Croaking some nonsense to yourself which soon
May escape your puffing cheeks with sudden plop.
Your's are the toga's words. Your skill it is
To join them in smooth phrases while your cheeks
Swell not too much. Your's the acquired skill
To scour our pallid mores while you nail
Our vices down with gentlemanly jest,
Drawn from the matters you would treat: forsake
Mycenae's feasts of heads and feet and learn
To know the tables of the common folk."
"My aim is surely not to load my page
With swollen nothings, to give weight to smoke.
I speak in confidence. To you I'd give
(Because the Muses will it so) my heart
To be explored, that you may know, dear friend,
How much of it is your's. So, strike it now,
Consider well how much of it rings true
And what is varnish on a painted tongue.
For this alone I crave a hundred voices,
To tell in clarion tones how fixed are you
Within the inmost contours of my soul,
To make my words unfold the secret truth
Which lies unspoken in my very heart."

Here, surely, in conversation with his friend and teacher, Cornutus, Persius is speaking sincerely and is using the style which
he approves. He begins with a carefully rhetorical opening: careful
use of anaphora, reminiscence of Homer, Vergil and Horace, and
a striking circumlocution for the epic, all in four lines. Incidentally,
the economy of words, in spite of the rhetoric, is unusual. There
are twenty-nine words to translate for which Mr. Connington used
fifty-seven. Granting Connington's generosity with words and the

lack of cases in English, the difference is still worth noting. Cornutus pulls him up sharply but again with an unusual and overstriking phrase: What are these great gobbets of song? He goes on to contrast the windy blasts of the tragedians with what Persius, as a satirist, should produce, the words of the toga, neat expression and moderate smoothness, capable of attacking vice like a gentleman. All of this indicates that Persius would have himself considered as in Horace's class: a writer of Satire, no bombastic rhetorician but a user of the common language. Yet, it is all put in an unnatural, figurative and highly strained style. "Skilled to scour our pallid mores" carries concise figure beyond the limit of ready comprehension.

Such is the light which Persius sheds on his own work. That work consists of five Satires (not counting the introductory first) all dealing with phases of Stoic philosophy. The second, fifth and sixth are addressed to specific friends of the poet without great relevance to the subject matter beyond a certain general suitability. In each case the Satire develops into a philosophic discourse without returning to the person addressed. Satire three treats in the same way an imaginary man of the decadent social class and the fourth Satire assumes a conversation between Socrates and Alcibiades about which not much can be said because of the fragmentary condition of the text. Persius never attained to the mastery of dramatic setting which marks Horace's second book of Satires. In the second Satire, after wishing Macrinus a happy birthday and assuring him that his prayers are worthy and will be heard by the gods, the poet berates the folly of mankind in praying for wealth, social position and long life and winds up with a few striking lines of more positive philosophy. (II.68–75.)

> Tell me, you priests, what use for gifts of gold
> Within your sanctuary? Just as much,
> I think, as for the dolls maids give to Venus.
> Let us give rather to the gods above
> What blear-eyed offshoots of Messala's line
> Can never bring; duty to god and man

Well blended and a mind within itself
At peace through generous nobility.
With these I'll make my prayer with simple meal.

Satires three and four deal with the life unmotivated by philosophy and public spirit. Number five, the most ambitious, is addressed to Cornutus and discusses true freedom which can come only with the acceptance and practice of true philosophy. The personal introduction, with its tribute to Cornutus already quoted, is extended to unusual length consistent with the greater extent of the satire as a whole. But the poet is ponderous in his approach to the central theme. With Horace in mind, he starts off with the varied ambitions of mankind. (V.52–61.)

A thousand human types there are and man
Behaves in multi-colored ways while each
Pursues his own desires, no two alike.
One trades Italian goods neath eastern sun
And brings back wrinkled pepper, cummin pale;
The next prefers to follow a full meal
With sluggish sleep; another joys in sport.
Gambling is one man's ruin, another's love.
But, when the storm of gout has cracked the joints
Like limbs of an old beech, too late they groan
For life departed with its fog-bound days.

At line 73, the real aim of life is stated and the real subject of the Satire: freedom. Not civil freedom but a freedom of will which only philosophy can give. The most vivid bits are two pictures, one of avarice and luxury pulling the young man in opposite directions, the other of the vaccillating lover. (V.161–168.)

"Davus, see here, I've seriously in mind
To end this wretched state," Charestratus
Affirms, biting to the quick his fingernails.
"Shall I disgrace my sober relatives
Forever? Ruin my fortune scandalously,

Singing my drunken songs at Chryses' door
With torch exhausted?" "Good, my boy, you're wise.
The gods have saved us: sacrifice a lamb."
"But, Davus, don't you think she'll weep for me?"

Persius would seem to have had in mind both the first Satire of Horace and the seventh of his second book but also he echoes several others. He is evidently making a serious effort to show Cornutus what he has absorbed of his Stoic teaching and also to produce an important Satire to rival his predecessor in the style of a new era. Needless to say, he does not wholly succeed but, in spite of obscurities, in spite of an un-Horatian impetuosity, there is vividness in his pictures and force in his earnest presentation.

These are undoubtedly the qualities which enabled the verses of Persius to survive. His lack of consistent form, his irritating obscurity and the roughness of his transitions are for the most part more conspicuous today than his real virtues which, with maturity, might well have given him greater stature. But his Stoic sincerity appealed to his particular group of friends and they were for the most part Stoics who came in one way or another into conflict with the government and whose writings were preserved by later admirers. Furthermore, in spite of his scorn of the pretty writers of contemporary verse, he wrote in the intense style of the exhibitionists of his day and in the story of first century literature he is of singular importance as representing the transition from Augustan poetry to that of the Flavian era.

The sixth and last Satire of the collection, on the proper use of wealth, is less grimly Stoic than the others, but Persius takes pains to indicate that he is not transgressing the bounds of his creed, only lending it a somewhat more human interpretation. It is therefore interesting to note that the text of the discourse is from the second Epistle of Horace's second book, lines 190–192: "I shall spend and I shall take from that little hoard what the occasion requires nor shall I fear what my heir shall judge of me because he does not find more than what is given him." The unusual use of *utar* in an absolute sense adds sure confirmation to the argument from similarity of thought as does also, to a lesser degree, the first

word of the Satire, *acervo,* something of a favorite with Horace
and used by him in this particular passage. From these various
considerations and from the fact that the sixth Satire seems never
to have been finished, it is likely that it was the last one composed
and may therefore be fairly considered as typical of Persius' best
work. I therefore quote it in full.

> Has winter moved you, Bassus, to your farm?
> Already do your lyre's strings ring forth
> Beneath your austere quill? Artist you are
> That wakes to music our primaeval tongue,
> The virile utterance of the Latin harp—
> Artist that presently in honored age
> With seemly thumb will pluck the chords that rouse
> The youth to festive love. For me today
> Liguria's shore is warm and winter's sea
> Is at its best where barrier cliffs reach far
> Until the shore recedes in one great bay.
> "Citizens, know it well, tis worth your pains,
> The port of Luna"—so great Ennius' heart
> When he had waked from dreamt Maeonides
> And from the peacock of Pythagoras.
>   Here I, with never a care for the mad crowd,
> Or for the south wind threatening the flocks,
> Or for my neighbor's plot richer than mine
> Though all the lesser born grow rich apace,
> Will still refuse to bow before old age
> Or dine with never a dainty or yet thrust
> My nose into a bottle of sour wine.
> Others may disagree. Old horoscope,
> You bring forth twins of opposite intent.
> You'll see a man who, at his birthday feast,
> Seasons dry vegetables with brine that's bought
> By cupful, sprinkles pepper sparingly
> By hand; another, lordly in his youth,
> With lusty tooth consumes a fortune vast.
> I'll spend my wealth, I swear, but not to serve

Freedmen with turbot nor to gain the skill
Of testing shrewdly juices of female thrush.
　　Live to the limit of your harvestings
And grind the contents of your granaries.
Why fear? Another crop will follow fast.
"But duty calls me, for a shipwrecked friend
Hangs helpless on the Bruttian cliffs. His all,
In wealth and prayers, the Ionian Sea devours
While he lies on the shore and by him there
The vessel's gods, and now the gulls collect
About the shattered wreckage of the ship."
Well now, break off a bit of your green turf
And give the poor man something that he may
Escape the fate of wandering with his board
Painted in ocean hues. "But" you object,
"My heir will skimp my funeral feast in wrath
At capital lost: he'll put my bones to rest
Ill scented while he wilfully ignores
Spoiled spice and cassia mixed with cherry bark.
You'd cut your fortune without penalty?
And Bestius blames the Greek philosophers:
'This is what comes of wisdom brought to town
Unpickled, with the spices and the palms:
Our hayseeds drench their mush with gummy oil.'"
Can this disturb you when you're turned to ash?
　　But you, *my* heir, whoever you may be,
Listen to this in private. My good man,
Haven't you heard that laurel wreaths are come
From Caesar for his glorious victory
Over the German youth: our altars now
Are being readied while Caesonia
Lets bids for arms to deck the temple doors
And royal robes with yellow garb as well
For captives, chariots and mighty Rhines.
I too am ordering me a hundred pair
Of gladiators, honoring the Prince
For his great deeds. Dare now to bid me nay.

Bad luck to you if you object. I'll give
Donations to the mob of oil and meat.
Do you forbid? Speak up. You'll not accept
What I bequeath? Well, here's a field
Already cleared of bones. If I've no aunts
Paternal left nor cousins to succeed,
No great niece and my mother's sister's dead,
(No issue there) and all my granddame's line
Are gone, why then, off to Bovillae, I
Or off to Vibius' height where, ready-made
As heir, some Manius waits. "A son of earth?"
Who was my fourth grandsire? Come, ask me that.
Though not off-hand, I still can say. Go back
One step, and then one more: we'll come at last
To some rude son of earth. So Manius proves
Quite properly an uncle of some sort.

    Now why should you, next runner in the race,
Demand my torch before I've finished? Mine
The role of Mercury to you. I come a god
As he's depicted: will you take my gift,
Accept with gratitude what's left? "Some bit
Is missing." Yes, I spent it for myself;
For you, what's left is all. Stop questioning
In fatherly tones what Tadius left me once.
"Add up the interest, deduct expense:
What's left?" What's left? Come, boy, douse with good oil
The cabbage. Damn expense. Shall I make glad
On nettles this fair day and a split pig's ear,
That *your* young, good-for-nothing heir may feast
On lights and liver of a goose, the while
He palpitates with passion and deflowers
Some fair patrician? Am I then to die
A skinny relic while his stomach swells?

    Go, sell your soul for gain. Go, trade with wiles
In every land; let none more shrewdly slap
Fat Cappadocians on the auction block.
Double your fortune. "So I've done: three times

As much, nay, four, nay, ten comes to my purse.
Mark it where I shall stop." Chrysippus, see:
We've found the man to end your endless heap.

The opening lines, addressed to his poet friend, Caesius Bassus,
are not only reminiscent of Horace but approach the authoritative
Horatian touch. The later poet is, however, less impressed with
the atmosphere of his retreat than with the literary note to which
it gives occasion: Ennius had been there and inspires a semi-
learned reference to two stages of his transmigratory career. The
picture of the shipwrecked friend of the interlocutor (Bassus is
well-nigh forgotten) is, even if exaggerated, still more or less
conventional. The reference to Bestius is sufficiently puzzling, the
Greek philosophers are irrelevant. Bestius appeared in Horace
(Epist. II. 15. 37.) where he also seems out of place and has
caused the commentators infinite trouble. He may have been proverbial, possibly stemming from Lucilius, and may have made
sense to contemporary readers. That Persius borrows him directly
from Horace is to some degree confirmed by what seems to be
another echo of the same epistle. Persius' *bona dente / grandia
magnanimus peragit puer* vaguely suggests Horace's *rebus maternis
atque paternis / fortiter absumptis*. The Epistle and the Satire both
deal with the winter retirement of the author to the pleasant shore
resorts and there is similarity in the detailed indications of rich
and mean fare and each has a rather obscure reference to the
Stoic puzzle called *sorites*: how many grains make a pile?

It is fairly clear that, while Persius felt himself to be heir to the
tradition of Lucilius and Horace (even to the point of accepting
the pedigree which Horace set up of Eupolis, Cratinus and Aristoph-
anes) and while he took issue in matters of taste and style with
his poet contemporaries, nevertheless he reflects vividly many
characteristics of a new and almost revolutionary style. In this he
furnishes the critic with an example, not exactly of the first century
manner but of the elements of that manner and of the transition to
it of the manner of the Augustan Age.

The atmosphere of the earlier period had been one of peace and
satisfaction. More than that, the Augustan poets showed a serene

confidence which resulted from their mastery of the art. Whether they dealt with serious matters of national import or with the more frivolous affairs of the individual, they wrote with that surety of touch which marks the master artist. In contrast with this calm self-confidence the poets of the following century show a nervous insecurity, a striving for effect which results often in brilliancy but equally often in extravagance of expression, lack of dramatic unity and an underlying tone of anxious distrust. Persius did not live long enough to produce any masterpiece of this new type. But the very lack of maturity, with its naïve and puzzling results, enables us to see clearly one of the prime sources of at least the more superficial characteristics of the newer poetry. He was still sufficiently under the influence of the rhetor's school and its offshoot, the social recitation, to exhibit plainly their trend toward exhibitionism. At the same time, with his youthful enthusiasm and sincerity of purpose, he left behind him an unforgetable impression of the basic integrity of that philosophy which underlay the struggle against the tyranny of imperialism and the moral inconsequence of a corrupt society.

CHAPTER FIVE

Lucan

PERSIUS'S CONTEMPORARY and fellow student, Marcus Annaeus Lucan, stands out in sharp contrast with the satirist both as an individual and as a writer. Lucan was violently concerned with politics, finally meeting his end in the Pisonian conspiracy against Nero, and he had an inborn sense of the poetic which Persius lacked. But, in a different medium and with a different spirit, he illustrates clearly the influences which dominated both these young writers. Lucan, like Persius, died before he was thirty.

Lucan was the nephew of Seneca, the Stoic philosopher, and was brought from Spain to Rome as a child. Born in 39 A.D., he was already known as a successful poet when he was twenty-one. Five years later he had been quaestor, was a member of the college of augurs, had defeated the emperor Nero in a poetry contest, had joined enthusiastically in the conspiracy to assassinate Nero. He had paid the death penalty for his rashness after a melodramatic exhibition of cowardice and bravado. During this period he had written ten books of the *Pharsalia*, his surviving epic on the civil war between Caesar and Pompey, as well as miscellaneous poems of which we have some twenty titles but none of which survive to-day. It was a feverishly active five years, filled with emotional crises.

Lucan's premature start in the political arena was undoubtedly due to the position of his uncle as chief adviser to the emperor. Seneca, first tutor, then counsellor to Nero, had long walked a political tight rope in his attempt to maintain his privileged position with his imperial pupil. He himself came from a conservative provincial family. The philosophical essays which he had published and some of which were surely intended for Nero's study expounded the principles of Stoic faith. His tragedies (which may have been only privately circulated) were full of Stoic dogma and epigram, denouncing the tyrant and lauding the ideal king. When his diplomatic compromises went so far as to defend Nero's murder of his mother, his influence began to fail. He shortly lost his advisory position and was eventually purged on the charge of participation in the conspiracy which proved fatal to Lucan. The young nephew must have been in a precarious position throughout his meteoric career. Trained in the Stoic school under Cornutus, he was nevertheless essentially a poet. Even a rhetorical poet who has authentic poetic genius is likely to be emotionally tense. Lucan's emotionalism verged on the psychotic.

It is not strange that such a temperament and such experiences should have led Lucan to choose for his epic the subject which he selected. The group in which he was brought up and with whom he was always in touch believed in the old republic with a tenacious fanaticism which gave to it an unrealistic aura of perfection. The depiction of Caesar as the headstrong and ruthless individualist and of Pompey as the guardian of Roman tradition was congenial to the young rebel who had been slighted by the inheritor of Caesar's power. The history of the *Pharsalia* was near enough to contemporary affairs and sufficiently related to them to offer thrilling material and yet far enough removed to avoid immediate danger. Historical epic was not a new thing at Rome but it had not achieved success since the days of Ennius, and Lucan could feel that he was blazing a new trail. Guided by his Stoic beliefs, he made a further new departure by banishing the gods from his epic, the gods who to him as to Tacitus had no interest in the affairs of men save that of punishing their folly. Human causes motivate the action of the *Pharsalia,* not the jealousies and whims of the gods.

The *Pharsalia* begins with Caesar's arrival in Italy from Gaul. He is still in the neighborhood of Rimini when the first book ends with a description of the terror in Rome magnified by omens and dire prophecies. Caesar and Pompey have been duly portrayed. Book II introduces Brutus and Cato and carries the story through Pompey's departure from Brindisi for Greece. The siege of Massilia is the chief subject of the third book and the fourth deals with minor engagements in Spain, Illyria and Africa. Book V begins with Pompey and the friendly senate in Epirus and ends with Pompey's separation from his wife, Cornelia. The central part of this book is occupied largely with the storm during which Caesar crosses the Adriatic. Book VI is concerned with minor actions and contains an extended description of Thessaly and its witches. The battle fills the seventh. Book VIII carries Pompey to Egypt and his death. In Book IX Cato conducts the remnants of the republican army across the African desert which is described at length with a catalogue of its snakes. The unfinished tenth book deals with Caesar at Alexandria.

Such is the bare outline of the history contained in the *Pharsalia*. There is no all inclusive unity of plan such as there was in the *Aeneid* nor does the sheer power of the story carry it on resistlessly to a climax. Lucan does not rely on closely knit drama to hold his audience but rather on a long series of brilliant descriptions, incidents, speeches and novelties designed to thrill a series of audiences. The wholly or partially irrelevant interludes in the direct narrative are more indicative of the character of the literary creation than the narrative itself and it is these which must be scrutinized to gain an understanding of the author as a product of his age.

It will be best to look first at the launching of the story. Homer and Vergil had plunged almost immediately into the stories they had to tell with only the briefest of appeals to the Muse for assistance and just enough of the immediate background to orient their stories. Lucan reveals himself at once as more prolix and more philosophical, more analytical and less objective. He ignores the Muse, probably as one who would be ill at ease in the midst of economic discussion and civil strife. He himself acts as showman of his own performance.

> Wars more than civil wars I celebrate
> Fought o'er Emathian plains, crime justified,
> A mighty people with victorious hand
> Turned on itself, lines of embattled kin

And, with the severance of the tyrants' pact,
A conflict of the universe itself
Rushing to common guilt: standards opposed
To standards, eagles matched and Roman pikes
Drawn against Roman pikes.
What madness this, oh fellow citizens,
What lust of war, to offer Latian blood
To be the joy of hated foreigner?
And when proud Babylon was still unspoiled
Of rich Ausonian trophies, while the ghost
Of Crassus wandered unavenged, could you
Choose to wage war no triumph could adorn?
Alas, what vast domain of land and sea
Might have been won by blood so freely shed
By fellow citizens: whence Titan comes
And where Night beds his stars and where midday
Burns with its blazing hours, where the grim cold
Of everlasting winter, knowing no spring,
Makes stiff the icy sea with Scythian frost;
Beneath our laws the Seres now had come,
Barbarous Araxes too and unknown folk
That dwell beside the sources of the Nile.
Then, Rome, if such your will to impious war,
When you have bent the world to Latian Laws,
Then turn against yourself. As yet we lack
Not enemies.
That now the cities of our Italy
Lie ruined heaps where walls and towers stood,
Our homes unguarded, while the rare citizen
Roams empty towns of old, Hesperia,
O'ergrown with thistles and unploughed for years,
Calls vainly for the hands to till her fields.
Not thou, proud Pyrrhus, art the cause
Of such destruction, not thou, Hannibal:
No stranger's sword has e'er so fatally
Struck home: deep lie the wounds of civil strife.

These lines are followed by a fulsome address to Nero. If the way for *his* coming could be arranged by Fate only through the vast disasters of civil war then the writer makes no complaint. The eulogy continues for over thirty lines with almost farcical extravagance and Nero is accepted as the muse for the poem. The rhetorical exaggeration is enough to have strained even Nero's credulity. It may be that Lucan merely follows the trend of the day, characteristically overdoing the complimentary address, but it is hard to believe that there is not a bitter irony beneath the surface flattery. When the poet places Nero in heaven, his mortal work done, and bids him choose his place at heaven's center that he may not throw the cosmos out of balance, he not only creates a ludicrous picture but is inconsistent with his own repudiation of the emperor cult elsewhere in the poem. (Cf. VI.809, VII.455, VIII.835, etc.)

From this rhetorical outburst Lucan turns to the exposition of the causes of the civil war which he had denounced in the earlier lines. (I.67–86.)

My mind is moved to expound the hidden springs
Of those great deeds: a mighty task unfolds.
What drove the maddened populace to arms?
The jealous course of Fate, laws that forbid
The greatest things long to endure, collapse
Supreme beneath a greatness overgrown,
A Rome too great which could not brook itself.
So, when the complex of our universe
Resolves, and to its countless centuries
The last hour sounds, old Chaos reigns again,
Then all the constellations of the sky
Shall clash confounded, stars shall seek the sea
And earth no more push forward with her shores
To fend the ocean. Phoebe shall turn and drive
Across her brother's course, claiming as her's
The paths of day and all earth's shattered frame
Shall rend the universe with anarchy.

> All greatness breeds collapse, a limit's set
> By law divine to new prosperity.
> For Fortune tempers not her jealousy
> For any race against a folk grown great
> By land and sea. Thou, Rome, thou wert the cause
> Of all our ills when thou hadst once become
> The common property of masters three
> Under a compact fraught with tyranny
> Nor e'er submitted to the public vote.

Here is a mixture of philosophy and history, of rhetoric and politics, a mixture found throughout the *Pharsalia* and typical both of Lucan's confused and unsettled mind and of the equally distraught age in which he lived. For the moment, history prevails. After a sketchy account of the triumvirate and of Crassus' elimination, bringing Caesar and Pompey face to face, Lucan proceeds, in accord with historical tradition, to present character sketches of the two leaders. But it is rhetorical history which he follows, not the tradition of a Livy. For the purpose of his contrast he exaggerates the difference in age between the two leaders. The young, impetuous and fearless Caesar was already fifty-two in the year of Pharsalus and Pompey, the aged, worn-out veteran was only six years older. The balanced and extended similes have also the flavor of the rhetor's school. There is, however, no question of the effective brilliance of the two sketches, sketches which have justly received the world's acclamation ever since Lucan's day. The translator can only blush at the results of reproduction in English.

> Not equal did they meet. One with his years
> Close to old age, long in civilian garb,
> Had now unlearned in peace the arts of war
> And, seeking office yielded to the voice
> Of popular acclaim, his ear attuned
> To the applause that echoed from the walls
> Of his own theater, building no new strength
> But trusting to the fortune of the past,
> He stands the shadow of a mighty name.

As in some fruitful field an ancient oak
Supports the trophies of a people's might,
The dedications of its chiefs. It stands
Spreading its empty branches to the air,
Its gaunt trunk offering only leafless shade.
And though it sways with every fickle breeze,
Threatening to fall while all the woods around
Are filled with sturdier trees, still it alone
Is held in reverence. Not such the name
Of Caesar, hero born by fate to lead,
Whose valor cannot rest, whose only shame
Is not to win in war. Alert, unchallenged,
Always in action, sparing no rash assault,
Pressing his own success and challenging
The favor of the gods, thrusting aside
All that would bar his passage to the peak;
Leaving a trail of ruin in his wake.
As when the lightning bolt from out the clouds
Flashes with din of universal blast,
Bursting the day asunder, frightening
The trembling populace, with darting flame
Blinding their eyes, raging against its own
Domains and unopposed spreads holocaust,
Coming and going, only to collect
Again its scattered fires.

The introduction is not yet complete. Lucan has a further
explanation to offer. This today would be called the economic
background of the war.

Such passions moved the leaders but beneath
Lurked public seeds of war, the eternal cause
Of shipwreck to the mightiest powers of earth.
For when, the whole world conquered, Fortune gave
Uncounted wealth, when character succumbed
To high prosperity, when plunder taught
The ways of luxury with no limit set

To gold-decked houses, when new hunger spurned
The frugal board, then men bedecked themselves
With garb effeminate; frugality,
The nurse of heroes, fled and from the ends
Of earth men sought the universal curse.
Then field was joined to field and what of old
Camillus furrowed, acres that once had felt
The plowshares of the Curii, now emerged
Neath absent landlords. This was not a folk
Whom grateful peace could lure, whom liberty
Could satisfy without recourse to war.
Thence ready anger and, beneath the goad
Of poverty, crime became cheap, man's goal
To outstrip in power the fatherland. So force
Became the gauge of justice. Thence decrees
Passed under durance, tribunes and consuls joined
To upset the laws, the fasces bought and sold,
The people fawning on its own patronage.
Corruption, ever fatal to the state,
Controlled the elections at the polls.
Next came devouring debt with interest
That pawned the future, credit itself destroyed
And, for the many, no recourse but war.

And so, at line 183, the scene is set for the opening of the action. Once more it is delayed, this time by the vision of protesting Rome which comes to Caesar as he approaches the fateful crossing of the Rubicon. But this vision is part of the narrative as are the omens and prophecies at the end of Book I and elsewhere. The introduction proper ends with line 182. It has been on the whole philosophical in content and rhetorical in manner with definite elements of the method of prose history. The summary of events leading up to the coming action and the sketches of the leaders are, when allowance is made for the poetic medium, midway between the style of Livy and that of Tacitus. The Stoic belief in foreordained Fate and the Stoic dogma that wealth and prosperity are the root of most evils are constantly to the fore. The persistence of the personal angle, the urge to interpret and comment, is equally prominent. These elements are characteristic of the epic as a whole and serve to make of it something wholly different from the *Aeneid*, something which must be judged and appreciated, not in comparison with Vergil's dramatic epic, but on its own merits. It is undoubtedly the masterpiece of rhetorical epic and as such has exercised a great influence on later ages. Nor are its qualities difficult of definition.

These qualities emerge clearly as soon as the narrative proper gets underway with line 183 of the first book. It is perhaps best to quote the entire fifty lines which tell of the crossing of the Rubicon and the march on Rimini.

> Caesar by now had pierced the frozen Alps
> And in his heart had formed the mighty plan
> Of war to come. But when he reached the stream
> Of little Rubicon a vision met
> The general's gaze, his trembling fatherland,
> Bright in the shades of night and sad of mien,
> With hoary locks dissheveled neath a crown
> Of turrets, and with groans addressed him thus:
> "Where lies your goal? Where march my banners brave?
> If with good right you come as citizens
> Only so far your right." Horror benumbed
> The leader's limbs, his hair stood up on end
> And terror froze him at the river's bank.
> Ere long he spake: "Thou mighty Thunderer
> That from the Tarpeian Rock dost watch the walls
> Of lordly Rome and ye Penates brought
> From Troy to bless the Julian family,
> Ye secret rites of old Quirinus, thou
> Jupiter Latiaris on the heights
> Of Alba throned, of Vestal hearthfires too
> And Rome, embodiment of divinity,
> Bless my emprise. Not with a madman's arms
> Do I this day attack you; lo, I come,
> Victor by sea and land, Caesar, even now,

If so ye will, your faithful champion.
His the foul guilt who makes of me your foe."
No more delay but through the swollen stream
He led his eagles as on the squalid plain
Of torrid Africa when the lion sees
His foe approaching, first he hesitates,
Collects his wrath, with lashing tail whips high
His fury, bristles his tawny mane and roars
To heaven, then, as the swift thrown Moorish lance
Pierces his flank or as the hunter's spear
Tears his broad chest, oblivious of the wound,
He breaks his way through the encircling steel.

From gentle springs with softly flowing stream
The Punic Rubicon slips on its way
In summer's blazing heat, winding about
Through lowly valleys, marking the boundaries
Twixt Gaul and farmlands of Ausonia.
But now the winter gave it strength, the third
Cynthia raised its waters and the Alps,
Dissolved by Eurus' blasts, pregnant with rain.

So first the cavalry in slanting line
Is placed against the river's pushing force;
Through milder shoals follow the troops on foot,
Breasting the waters of the humbled stream.
When Caesar then had reached the farther bank
And stood upon Hesperia's shore, denied
To him by law, he halted. Then he spake:
"Here I take leave of peace, abandon law,
To follow Fortune's lead. Let compacts fall.
I put my faith in Fate: war be my judge."
Straight on these words the tireless general
Beneath the shades of night advanced with speed
Like that of Balearic missile or the shaft
From treacherous Parthian bow, against the town
Of Rimini just as the rising sun

Scattered the stars in flight. The day began
Destined to see the first tumult of war.

This first narrative passage in the *Pharsalia* consists of some
fifty lines. At most, ten of these can be called narrative; the rest
comprise a vision, a longer and a shorter speech, an extended
simile and a bit of poetic description. The proportions are not far
from those which prevail throughout the epic. The reader becomes
familiar with phrases indicating the return to narrative: *iam
Caesar, Caesar ut, interea, iamque.* Major digressions form at least
a fifth of the whole work. These are partly geographical: the topog-
raphy of Italy (II.394–438), of Thessaly (VI.333–412), of Libya
(IX.411–497); partly displays of learning: astronomy: (IV.48–86,
IX. 528–543), navigation: (VIII.165–201), the oracle at Delphi:
(V.65–120), Thessalian magic: (VI.452–569), the snakes of Africa: (IX.619–838); partly rhetorical exercises in description: the
Druids' grove: (III.399–452). One is a long historical digression
on Marius and Sulla (II.67–233) and another a tale from mythology, the story of Antaeus (IV.590–660). Certain features of prose
history which slow down the narrative but which were accepted as
normal are, by their rhetorical expansion or exaggeration, more
conspicuous in Lucan's poetical treatment: omens, visions, prophecies, speeches characterizing a situation or a man, catalogues of
forces. The moralizing, such as appeared in the introduction and
which reappears constantly throughout the epic, often with exclamatory appeal, is more strictly rhetorical. The most striking case
of moralizing reflexion is the section in the seventh book (385–
459) on the significance of the battle.

So then on either side with equal rage
The lines push forward: fear of tyranny
Compelling these, the hope to win it those.
Their hands shall do what ageless time could not
Nor humankind in any span of years:
Make obsolete the sword. That battlefield
Shall put an end to nations yet unborn
And peoples of the future, blotting out

Their natal day. Then every Latin name
Shall be a story told, when Gabii,
Veii and Cora shall be recognized
Only as ruins buried in the dust.
The Alban lares and the Laurentian gods
Shall dwell in barren wastes inhabited
By none save that unwilling senator
Forced in the dead of night to carry out
Numa's decree. No ravages of time
Have thus reduced those monuments of old:
Tis civil crime has laid these cities low.
To what is now reduced the human race?
We who survive on earth can never fill
Its city walls or countryside. One town
Holds all of us. By captive slaves are raised
Hesperian crops where stands the crumbling house
With none to fall on. Rome, deserted now
Of all its citizens, filled with the dregs
Of earth, we have consigned to such a fate
That none is left to foster civil war.
Such evil hath Pharsalia wrought. Let now
The fatal name of Cannae and the blot
Of Allia on Rome's fasti yield their crown.
Rome signalized her days of lighter woe:
This she would fain not know. Ah, cruel Fate!

This is only half of the passage. It goes on to mourn the fact
that Pharsalia has reversed all Roman history: India is set free
from anxiety as are the Dahae, the Sarmatians, the Parthians. Liberty has retreated beyond the Rhine and the Tigris. Rome would
have been better off never to have known liberty. So the poet
would complain of the Brutus clan of liberators. All this is an-
ticipatory reflection: the battle is still to come. It plays the part of
omens or prophecy in rhetorical epic or of the motivating ghost in
rhetorical drama. It prepares the listening audience for the horrors
to come.

This tone-setting function of long passages which are not wholly

irrelevant but which interrupt the flow of the narrative tends to
become monotonous and would be completely boring if it were not
for Lucan's ability to create variety even in the midst of monotony
and to produce brilliant epigrammatic phrases to command attention. The close similarity to Seneca is obvious. Lucan does not
show the dramatic qualities of unity and character development,
so conspicuous in the *Aeneid*, but in this area the resemblance to
Seneca is suggestive. Vergil was inspired by the tragedy of Sophocles, Lucan by the very different type represented by Seneca. The
terms drama and melodrama are too vague and overloaded with
modern connotation but they serve to indicate a very real difference between plots developed before and after the triumph of
school rhetoric. This is true both of plays intended for acting and
those intended for recitation.

The opening of Book II is typical of Lucan's procedure. He
begins with some fifteen lines of grim reflection on omens and
hope, then launches into fifty lines of protest against civil war. This
last is put into the mouth of a citizen departing for camp but the
illusion is weak: it is Lucan who speaks throughout.

> Now was the wrath of heaven disclosed, the signs
> Of war made manifest, the established laws
> And compacts of the universe o'erthrown
> With vast confusion. Nature that foresaw all
> Disclosed the crimes to come. Why must thou add,
> Lord of Olympus, to our mortal woes
> This final bane, to know by omens dire
> Disasters still to come? Whether the sire
> Of all, when first from out the receding fires
> He seized and framed the shapeless mass,
> Fixed for eternity the laws that bind
> Creator and created, fettering fast
> The universe beneath the rule of Fate
> Or if instead naught here is permanent
> And Chance uncertain, wavering in its course,
> Rules the affairs of men, whate'er it be
> Thou hast in store for man, grant that it come

Unheralded. Let man be blind to fate
And while he trembles grant him still to hope.

*****

(Women are gathered at a shrine, bewailing the horrors of war to
come. One of them frantically addresses the rest.)

"Now, wretched mothers, beat your breasts and tear
Your tresses: wait not on the ills to come,
Postponing grief. Now you have power to weep
While fortune wavers; when one man prevails
You will perforce rejoice." So spake her grief.
Not less the men, as to the opposing camps
They made their way, poured forth their just complaints
To cruel gods. "Oh, we of bitter fate
That were not born to bear the Punic scourge
Of Cannae or of Trebia! Not peace we ask,
Ye gods above. Breathe into foreign folk
New wrath; rouse every barbarous power
Until the whole world wars as one on Rome.
From Achamenian Susa let the Mede
Pour forth in battle line, Hister no more
With Scythian flood restrain from massacre
The Massagetes; from the farthest north
Let Albis and the Rhone's unconquered source
Pour forth the Suevi with their tawny locks:
Make every race the enemy of Rome.
But spare us civil war. Let Dacian host
Beset us here, the Getae there, one chief
Lead us to battle Spain, the other bear
Rome's eagles 'gainst the quivers of the East.
Let none, oh Rome, be free to ravage thee.
Or if, ye gods, it be your will to end
Hesperia's name, then let the mighty breath
Of heaven's ether, gathering its fiery force,
Descend to earth in fiery thunderbolt.
Oh cruel sire, ere yet they consummate

Their guilt, strike both, leaders and hosts alike.
With such a harvest of unheard of crimes
Shall they decide which one shall rule the world?
Twere scarcely worth the price of civil war
That neither one should rule."

Such settings and such tonal monologues are frequent throughout the ten books of the epic. One variant is the account of Pompey's dream before the beginning of the battle at the opening of
Book VII. A more dramatic method of inducing vicarious horror
or dread is used in such a scene as that of Brutus consulting Cato
as to the proper course for him to follow in the dread crisis. Between the passages just quoted and this scene in Cato's house
there has intervened a long presentation of the despairing citizens
discussing the dreadful situation. It turns out to be one long speech
(over 150 lines) by an old man recalling the horrors of civil war
in the past. By the time he has finished, the three approaches em-
ployed by Lucan, reflection, exclamatory monologue and slightly
more dramatic exposition, have produced the picture of popular
confusion and dread. Hence the sharp contrast produced at line
234 when the scene changes from the public square to the house
of Cato. The new approach proves, however, to be only another
and more intellectual presentation of the dreadfulness of the crisis.

But helpless terror shattered not the heart
Of noble Brutus: in such panic fear
He did not join the grieving populace
But in the hours of sleep when Helice
Turned in its course her chariot, he knocked
Upon the humble door of Cato's home,
His kinsman Cato, whom he found immersed
In sleepless thought about the public weal,
The fate of man and of the city too,
Concerned for all yet sure of his own self.
So Brutus spake him: "You who are alone
The champion of Virtue, now from earth
Banished long since (and yet no dreadful blast

Of Fortune can dislodge her from your breast),
Do you direct me in my troubled state
With your unwavering strength. For some shall choose
To follow Magnus, others shall elect
The arms of Caesar: Cato alone shall be
Brutus' commander. Do you follow peace
With footsteps certain in a dubious world?
Or will you share the leaders' crimes, the fate
Disastrous of mad citizens, and so
Give absolution even to civil war?

*****

So, if you choose to take up arms to save
Your country's laws, to safeguard Liberty,
Brutus is your's, not as the enemy
Of Pompey or of Caesar, but the foe
Of him who wins the war." He ceased and from
His deepest soul came Cato's weighty words.
"The gods shall bear the guilt of making me
Guilty with all the rest. Yet who would watch
The stars of heaven fall, the universe
Collapse, himself untouched by danger? Who,
When upper ether rushed to earth's last day,
Would sit with folded hands? Shall unknown tribes
Support Hesperian madness and the wars
Of Rome and kings beyond the farthest seas
Neath other stars, while I alone withdraw
In peace? Such madness, gods above, forbid,
That Rome involved the Dahae in her fall,
The Getae too, while I remain secure.
As a fond father who has lost his son
Impelled by grief orders the funeral train
Wind slowly to the tomb, with his own hand
Applies the torch, kindling the heaped up pyre,
So I will not be torn away, beloved Rome,
Till I have clasped thy corpse, till to the name
Of Liberty and to its empty shade
I've done my duty."

Lucan also calls to his aid his power of description which can be made to serve the purpose of tone setting and is so used in his most quoted pen picture, that of the grove of the Druids at Massilia. Nature, strongly buttressed by imagination and sentimentality, is made to serve rhetoric just as Seneca used it in his Corsican lyrics but with infinitely more art and much more successfully. (III.399–425.)

There was a grove, of old inviolate,
Embracing with its interwoven boughs
A dim obscurity and shadows cool,
The sunlight far removed. This solitude
No rustic Pans, no forest wandering
Silanuses, no nymphs inhabited
But barbarous rites of strange divinities.
Altars were there with gruesome offerings
And every tree was bathed in human blood.
If we believe tradition's awestruck tales
No bird dare linger on those dreadful boughs,
No wild beast prowl beneath; no wind intrudes
Into those woods nor lightning from black clouds;
No trembling there of rustling foliage.
Full many a stream flows from benighted springs,
Weird images of gods, untouched by art,
Stand, shapeless blocks hewn from the trunks of trees.
The very site, the ancient lifeless mould,
Strikes terror in the worshippers: they fear
No powers dedicate by well known rites
But sense a greater terror, knowing not
What gods they fear. Rumor persuades them too
That hollow groans proceed from cavernous depths
That ancient beech trees, prone for ages, rise
To grow again while fires gleam everywhere
Though no woods burn and serpents coil about
The trunks of oak. No throngs frequent that grove:
Too dread the gods, and whether Phoebus drives
His chariot through the sky or black night rules

> The heavens, the priest himself dreads entering there
> And fears to approach the master of the grove.

One digression only in the *Pharsalia* deliberately tells the story of a myth. It is the tale of Antaeus and Heracles, told to Curio on his arrival in Africa by an old inhabitant to explain why the district was called the realm of Antaeus. This cannot be called a wholly irrelevant digression: it is introduced with some care in the natural course of the narrative. It has, however, a certain independent standing which gives it special interest. In twelve lines Curio arrives in Africa and pitches camp in what tradition calls the realm of Antaeus. He inquires of a native the reason for the name and then listens to the old man's story. At the end of the story there follow five lines (balancing the introductory twelve) in which Curio, delighted, accepts the story as a good omen for his African campaign. Incidentally the tale suggests the story of Cacus and Hercules told by Evander to Aeneas in the eighth book of the *Aeneid.* Vergil was the master story teller; Lucan's distinction lay elsewhere but he would seem to have taken a leaf at this point from the work of his predecessor. The Antaeus story is a very short epyllion set in a proper frame.

The geographical digression, giving some picture of new countries as they emerge to a position of prominence in the narrative, was a familiar element of prose history. It appears with considerable frequency in the *Pharsalia* where it is characterised by the same expansion and exaggeration as are the other types of digression, especially by its freight of learned information which smacks of the reference manual. The geography of Thessaly (VI.333ff.) is a striking example, winding up with a highly colored account of the Thessalian witches. Libya (IX.411ff.) furnishes the subject for another geographical essay which is thrown completely off balance by the catalogue of African snakes with which it concludes. A less extravagant example is the summary of Italian geography. (II. 399–429.)

> This ridge of mountain barrier lies midway
> Between the waters of the kindred seas

To east and west. Its guardian hills hold back
Here Pisa's Tuscan flood and, opposite,
Ancona, daring the Dalmatian waves.
Its rivers swell the paths of oceans twain:
In eastward course the swift Metaurus falls
And hurtling Crustuminium, Sapis, too,
Joined by Isaurus; Sena, Aufidus,
That lashes Adria's waters; mightiest
Of all, Eridanus sweeps to the sea
The wreckage of great forests with its floods
Draining Hesperia. Tradition tells
How once a poplar crown shaded her stream
And when with devious course in mad career
Phaethon drove the chariot of the day
With fiery reins kindling the air to flame
And earth was reft of its life-giving streams
This river only matched great Phoebus' fires.
Not less it were than Nile if Libyan Nile
Did not pursue its course through Egypt's sands
Not less than Hister save that Hister makes
Her way across earth's surface gathering
The waters of a host of springs and pours
By many mouths into the Scythian sea.
Westward the mountain springs, in downward plunge,
Create the Tiber and sheer Rutuba,
Next, swift Volturnus, Sarno with its breeze
By night, Liris with course that flows
Through lands of shadowy Marica's realm.
Fed by Vestinian springs, comes Siler next
Skirting Salerno's planted fields; above,
By woods unhampered, shallow Macra pours
Her waters seaward hard by Luna's walls.
Thence where the mountains with ascending ridge
Lift toward the heavens above, they look upon
The Gallic lands and rise to meet the Alps.

It is true that the epic of Lucan lacks structural unity. The parts

are developed at the expense of the whole. But the critic should be
on guard not to lose sight of another sort of unity which the
Pharsalia surely has and which gave it the appeal and power which
it undoubtedly exercised in the generation of Martial and again in
the days of Doctor Johnson. If our own taste is often offended by
the exaggeration of the component parts and if our admiration for
Vergil tends to make us critical of the passionate pomp of Lucan's
rhetoric, we are none the less, willingly or otherwise, swept resistlessly on by the tremendous pageant of the horror of civil war and
the tragic downfall of Liberty.

Again, when we say that Lucan wrote an historical epic, we
should remember that it is not alone to a Livy or an annalistic
historian that he could turn for his material. Lucan's history, in-
tensely passionate, burning with a partisan fury which never flags,
presumably had as a prose source a very different type of history.
Horace gives us a glimpse of such a history, perhaps the first of its
kind, composed in the third decade before Christ by Asinius Pollio.
He it was who originated the *recitatio* although he would not
"admit the public" to his readings. To him Horace addressed the
opening ode of his second book.

> The civil strife, launched in Metellus' year,
> The causes of that war, its villainies,
> The jests of Fortune and the compact dread
> Between three demagogues, the weapons donned
> Which still display unexpiated blood;
> You have essayed a task of monstrous chance
> For you are treading on the treacherous crust
> Above volcanic ash still smouldering there.

*****

> Already you assault our ears with blast
> Of trumpet and the bugles murmur threats;
> The gleam of arms already terrifies
> The fleeing horse and blanch the horseman's face.

> I seem to hear the cries of mighty chiefs

Rolled in the filthy dust inglorious
And all the wide world sunk to slavery
Save only Cato's proud, unyielding soul.

*****

What fields are not enriched with Latin blood
And with their graves testify impious war,
The ominous crash that farthest Media hears,
The eternal ruin of proud Hesperia?

What seas, what rivers have not heard the shock
Of that calamity? What ocean's brine
To-day is undefiled by Daunian dead?
What shores are still unwashed by Roman blood?

This is surely not the style of the contemplative Horace. He has been hearing the recital of a history far removed from the annals of Livy. Pollio must have written not only in partisan vein but with despair of the republic expressed in the rhetoric of a new age. Here is the key to Lucan's poem. The *causas belli,* the *ludum Fortunae,* the vicious triumvirate, the arms smeared with unexpiated blood, Cato alone emerging with any honor, the Parthians parading as Medes and Italy as Hesperia, all these appear in the introduction to the *Pharsalia,* all combine to set the tone of the epic. Pollio's history and Lucan's epic shared the element of horror at the downfall of an idealized republic. It was this atmosphere of consistent horror which gave to the poem its grandeur and such unity as it possessed.

The "sport of Fortune" is a substantial aid in producing the prevailing tone. This is of course a part of the Stoic element. At times Lucan, in his pessimism, almost confuses Fortune and Fate with mere Chance, but throughout the long poem it is malignant Fate which is punishing the Romans for their failure to maintain the old standard of Roman Virtue. When Pompey dies in Egypt, his spirit, purged of such ambition as he had had, leaves the tomb and flies to inspire Cato who can now fight sincerely for Liberty and Virtue only. It is Cato, the embodiment and symbol of

Stoicism, who continues the war and turns out to be the hero of
the poem. He is a tragic hero who will go down with the cause for
which he was forced to fight. (IX.1 ff.)

Yet not in Pharian embers did the soul
Lie buried: meagre ash could not contain
That mighty spirit. Bursting from the tomb,
Leaving its half burned corpse, the ignoble pyre,
It soared into the vault of thundering Jove
Where the dark ether laced by the speeding stars
Between the earth and Luna's lonely course
Receives the souls of heroes there to dwell,
Whose fiery virtue kept them free from guilt,
So to endure the lower range of air
Till they be gathered to their eternal realm.
There never come the spirits of the rich,
Buried in golden wealth and frankincense,
But thither wafted, clothed in purest light,
He marvelled at the constellations wheeling
In steadfast course, the stars that decked the heavens.
He saw what depths of darkness clothed our day
And laughed in scorn at his own mangled corpse.
Thence o'er Emathia's plains he soared aloft
O'er bloody Caesar's eagles, o'er the wrecks
Of scattered fleets and, as the avenging spirit
Of crimes committed, came to rest at last
Within the haven of Brutus' faithful heart
And in the unconquered soul of Cato dwelt.
Cato, while chance hung doubtful and no man
Could say whom civil war would certify
As master of the world, gave not his love
To Magnus, though his comrade sworn in arms
Obedient to his country's auspices
And bowing to the senate's will. But now
After Thessalia's rout, wholeheartedly
He stood Pompeian, and embraced the state
That lacked a champion, cared for the trembling troops,

Restored to cowardly hands the discarded sword,
Waging a civil war without desire
Of kingly power but willing still to serve.

The *Pharsalia* is an epic of Stoic tragedy in which the hero is
foredoomed and which ends in heroic disaster as do the Stoic
dramas of Seneca. On the part of a young man well under thirty,
involved in a political life of high tension, it was no slight achievement to produce an epic which has ever since been recognised as
perhaps the greatest creation of all time in the field of rhetorical
poetry.

CHAPTER SIX

Seneca

SENECA IS BEST KNOWN to the modern world as a philosopher. To his contemporaries he was a politician. But he was also a playwright and even fancied himself a lyric poet. In both lyric poetry and drama he is as thoroughly typical of the age of rhetoric and Stoic Satire as either Persius or Lucan. Lucius Annaeus Seneca, son of the rhetorician from Cordova and uncle of Lucan, was born about 3 B.C. and brought to Rome as a child. He was an enthusiastic student of rhetoric, frail of body but mentally precocious. With the backing of his maternal aunt whose husband was for sixteen years governor of Egypt, Seneca had a considerable success at the bar and a good start in politics. This career was interrupted in 41 A.D. when he was accused of indiscretions at court and banished to Corsica by Claudius at the instigation of Messalina. On the death of the emperor in 49, Agrippina secured Seneca's pardon and he returned to Rome to become the tutor of her son, the young Nero. When Nero became emperor Seneca continued to be his chief adviser and held this position for five years. His control over his headstrong pupil was lost when he consented to the defense of Nero for murdering his mother and he was eventually disposed of on the charge of participating in the conspiracy of Piso in 66.

The small collection of Seneca's early lyrics which has survived is of interest almost solely because of the light which they throw on the taste of the time and on the preoccupations of the writer. They are all as personal as the poems of Catullus but there is no further resemblance. Seneca's are pure rhetoric and therefore to us do not carry any conviction of sincere feeling, certainly none of inspired emotion. Those which deal with the Corsican period are, to be sure, freighted with despair and resentment, but the effect of the emotion is ruined by the burden of rhetoric.

> Shut in with cliffs, barbarian Corsica
> Lies waste and barren, horrid to behold:
> No fruits her autumn bears, summer no crops,
> And her white winters know not Pallas' gifts:
> No grateful shade bids welcome in the spring
> Her flocks, nor grassy meads neath summer's sun,
> No fields of grain she boasts, no dancing brooks:
> Two things are here, an exile, banishment.

The exaggeration and the straining after the point of the final line illustrate one characteristic which reappears continuously in these occasional lyrics. Another type of rhetorical usage, pedantic information, whether direct or by allusion, equally characteristic of the poems, appears most strikingly in the following:

> Corsica, settled of old by the wandering exiles of Phocis
> Corsica, erstwhile called Cydna by birthright forgot,
> Corsica, lesser by half than Sardinia, greater than Ilva,
> Corsica, traversed by floods, rivers that man travels not,
> Corsica, land to be feared when summer first scorches
>   the meadows,
> More to be dreaded by far, touched by the dog star's breath,
> Spare ye the banished from home, the exiles buried
>   though breathing,
> Light rest thy earth on these, living in worse than death.

One more product of the Corsican exile will be sufficient to show the effect of rhetorical training on the unhappy victim. It is a poem addressed to his native Cordova. After recalling the horrors which the town underwent during the civil war when it was "Pompey's foe and Caesar's too" the poet bids it grieve now for a greater tragedy.

I, I am ruined, thy once famous son,
Chained to a barren cliff. Oh, Cordova,
Rend all thy locks and thank what gods there be
That thou art washed by farthest ocean's waves.
So doth thy sorrow come less suddenly.

Stoic philosophy was the source of comfort to which Seneca turned both for himself and for his friends to whom he wrote consolatory essays from his Corsican retreat. He had studied it faithfully and is, in his prose writings, its most popular and reasonable exponent. But it seems to have afforded him little comfort even though he found some satisfaction in the conclusion that a greater holocaust awaited the world than had as yet befallen him personally.

Grim Time devours all things, evermore
Changes all things, leaves naught that's permanent.
The rivers fail, the sea leaves bare the shore,
Mountains are shattered, crags assunder rent.
And these are trifles: all the firmament
Of heaven above shall flame with sudden roar.
Death comes for all. Tis law, not punishment:
One day God's universe shall be no more.

In the meanwhile, while waiting for the final holocaust, Seneca states his determination to renounce the vicissitudes of a public career and to cultivate the simple life. This seems gratuitous on the part of a Corsican exile and, for a confirmed courtier, less than sincere, but the obvious rhetoric marks it as largely conventional.

Sooner the ships shall cease to sail the sea,
Sooner the quicksands fail on Libya's shore,
Sooner the melting snows desert the streams,
The Rhone no longer keep her southward course,
Sooner shall Corinth blend two seas in one
Nor battle with the doubly surging deep,
Sooner shall cruel lions yield in strife

To timid deer, the bear forget its might,
The Mede brandish the pike, the Roman youth
Don quiver, Indian locks take hue of flame
Than I forswear the joys of quietude
Or trust my barque out on a stormy sea.

Even more conventional are most of the lyrics: satiric epigrams, flattery of the emperor, poems on immortality won by poetry, (the Mausoleum and the pyramids play their wonted part) and trifles, friendly and vindictive, addressed to the poet's acquaintances. One of the longest of these approaches most nearly to natural sincerity, a poem on Hope. It has lines unaffected by exaggerated rhetoric or conventional philosophy.

Credulous still, that Fortune cannot fright,
Hope stands to serve us in our direst plight;
Hope contradicts us at the port of Death
When the kind sword would free our troubled breath.

This passage is, however, followed by a catalogue of the victims of Hope: Marius and Pompey, Priam and Protesilaus, Orpheus, Daedalus and Pasiphae, the farmer, the sailor, the fisherman and the hunter. And it all winds up with the epigram, *Hoc semper constans, quod fugit atque redit.*

The lyric efforts are of little importance save from two points of view. They indicate the nature of some of the fashionable verse being turned out in the various social circles of Rome of which Petronius offers other examples. Of more importance to the present discussion, they furnish a valuable background for a study of Seneca's nine tragedies which survived to make their indelible mark on the modern drama of Italy, France and England.

The plots of all of the plays are taken directly from the Greek, with Euripides as the most frequent source, but there the resemblance ends. These are no translations, not even close adaptations. One fundamental condition is in large part responsible for the complete difference between the Greek and the Latin creations. The Greek prototypes were written for production in the theater.

Their success in the great dramatic contests depended on their qualities as presented in action before an experienced and critical audience. The Roman plays on the contrary were written to be read or more probably recited before an invited audience. They show little or no regard for logical entrances and exits and contain scenes of gruesome horror impossible of presentation on the stage. They appeal to listeners trained in schools of rhetoric and looking for rich descriptions, vivid declamation, epigrammatic cleverness and raw emotional effects, preferably horrors. If, mingled with these, there were enough maxims of popular philosophy to lend an air of propriety, so much the better. Seneca, the disillusioned courtier, fed from childhood on rhetoric, gave what was wanted with lavish hand. As Lucan had shown the best of what rhetoric could make of the epic, so Seneca showed what rhetorical drama could be when created by an expert.

The prologue of a Sophoclean play began the action of the play, developed in realistic dialogue the opening situation and introduced one or more of the leading characters. Seneca, unconcerned with stage realism, usually opened with a long harangue, sometimes by one of the characters, sometimes by a god or a ghost, speaking directly to the audience, giving them the situation and especially the motivation for the action to follow. This speech by its tone regularly prepared the audience for the atmosphere of the play. The prologue speaker as a rule announced his own identity. The prologue is completely detached from the rest of the play. Historically, the transition from the Greek type of prologue to the Roman had been initiated by Euripides who sacrificed stage realism to a certain extent to speed and convenience in acquainting the audience with his plots, plots often less familiar than those of his predecessors and more concerned than their's with minor crises of life and its complications. Gods and ghosts were sometimes his speakers, for he was not averse to the spectacular. His prologue, however, while sometimes detached, did not have the rhetorical quality of Seneca's with their tone-setting function. Furthermore, in all but four of Euripides' plays, the opening speech is followed by a proper dramatic dialogue to complete the prologue.

This matter of tone production is fundamentally a product of rhetorical training. The manuals taught the orator to use the exordium or opening section of a speech for two purposes: first, to acquaint the judge and jurors with the nature of the case and, second, to make them attentive, amenable and well-disposed. These are the two functions of Seneca's prologues and the tone element is his means of rendering his hearers responsive to what follows.

Juno, in the *Hercules*, appears as a virago whipping herself (and the audience) into a frenzy of revenge.

> Up, wrath and on, crush the presumptuous churl
> That still aspires, tear him with thine own hands
> Nor leave thy will to others: let be wild beasts
> And all the Titan host. Dost seek a match
> For Hercules? There is but one—himself.
> With his own self let him wage war; call thou
> From lowest hell the stark Eumenides
> With flaming locks and in their savage claws
> Wielding the viper scourge. Go now, proud fool,
> And, scorning earth, assail the firmament.
> Dost think thou hast escaped the Stygian realm,
> The abode of shades? Here will I make for thee
> A very hell.

All of the learned astronomy which is crowded into the rest of this prologue cannot destroy the ferocity of it.

The *Medea* is, like the *Hercules*, a melodrama of revenge and fury. Medea herself is the source as well as the instrument of furious revenge. It is in this function of motivating rage (she is her own prologue ghost or divinity) that she speaks the opening harangue, first appealing to an array of baleful gods, including Hecate, Chaos, Hades and Persephone as well as the Furies, then invoking a curse upon Creon, Creusa and, with special fury, Jason. The latter half of the prologue is devoted to goading herself to the point of wreaking her mad revenge. In the *Oedipus*, the *Thyestes* and the *Agamemnon* the tone established in the prologue is one of undiluted horror. Oedipus himself, in a long monologue, sets the tone by the rhetorical picture of the pestilence.

> Banishing night, the uncertain sun returns,
> The dawn creeps up by squalid clouds oppressed
> And, with its baleful light of ominous flame,
> It shall disclose homes swept by greedy pest
> And day shall show destruction wrought by night.
> Joys any man in power? Oh treacherous boon,
> What ills with what fair seeming thou dost hide.

In the *Thyestes* and the *Agamemnon* the ghosts of Tantalus and Thyestes speak the prologues with grim reference to the accursed realm from which they rise to inspire the horror which pervades the two plays. A different tone was required for the *Troades,* an atmosphere of despair and woe and Hecuba is well fitted to produce the aura of hopeless tragedy.

> Whoso puts faith in might or rules supreme
> In royal halls nor fears the fickle gods,
> Yielding to pleasure with a credulous heart,
> Let him but look on me, ay look on Troy:
> Never hath Chance proven more ruthlessly
> How insecure the pinnacles of pride.

The changes which rhetoric effected in classical drama in the hands of Seneca are of particular interest to the English reader because it was Seneca's version which represented classical tragedy to Shakespeare and his immediate predecessors and which through them had a powerful influence on all English drama. Perhaps the most obvious of these changes was the reduction of natural dialogue in favor of longer speeches of one sort or another. In the Greek tragedies the dialogue carried the burden of plot development and, to a considerable degree, that of character presentation. It was the dominant element in every Greek play after the original choral character of Greek tragedy had been outgrown. In Senecan tragedy its function became very largely that of a vehicle for epigrammatic repartee. The difference is at once suggested by the proportionate space devoted by Euripides, for example, in his *Hippolytus,* to dialogue as compared with that alloted to it by

Seneca in his adaptation of the Hippolytus, the *Phaedra*. In the Greek play approximately 66% is dialogue, with only 22% devoted to longer speeches, including the messenger's speech reporting off-stage action. In Seneca's play the situation is roughly reversed, 21% dialogue and 55% longer speeches. And Euripides was the most rhetorical of the Greek dramatists with a weakness for extended descriptions and argumentative speeches.

A natural result of Seneca's use of the dialogue to appeal to his recitation audience was its failure to reproduce realistic conversation in which the parts were representative of the character speaking. All alike are apt to speak in the language of the rhetor's school, regardless of their position in the scale of culture. Medea's nurse bandies wise epigrams with her mistress with almost the same disregard of realism as that of the wounded sergeant in Macbeth who says so casually, "or memorise another Golgotha." A few lines will illustrate.

> *Nurse.* Tis hidden wrath hath power:
> Hate once disclosed has lost the power to strike.
> *Medea.* That grief is slight which can contain itself
> Or take advice. Great ills cannot be hid.
> I'll forward then. *N.* Come, check your mad impulse
> My child. Scarce secrecy can save you now.
> *M.* Fortune still fears the brave; cowards it slays.
> *N.* Try Fortune when there's room for bravery.
> *M.* Never shall there lack room for bravery.
> *N.* No hope reveals a way through your affairs.
> *M.* Who has no hope knows likewise no despair.

These lines are not extreme in their rhetorical tone but they illustrate a characteristic of Seneca's dialogue which was already familiar in Euripides but which the Roman playwright used more extravagantly: the picking up of a word used by the first character to be the key word of a striking phrase by the second. Pyrrhus and Agamemnon in the *Troades* (322 ff.) furnish a typical example of this practice.

P.   Twas then that mighty Hector, scorning your arms,
Trembled before Achilles' song: meanwhile
Deep peace there was amongst the Thessalian ships.
A.   Ay, and amongst those same Thessalian ships
There was deep peace for Hector's aged sire.
P.   Tis right a king give life unto a king.
A.   Why did your hand then rob a king of life?
P.   The merciful will oft give death for life.
A.   So, "merciful," you claim a virgin's life?
P.   Is it only now you fear a virgin's death?
A.   A king must put his throne before his child.
P.   No law protects a captive from her fate.
A.   What law forbids not shame may yet prevent.
P.   The victor may do whatsoe'er he will.
A.   Who may do most may well demand the least.

Too much use of this rapid fire, highkeyed repartee gives to a considerable portion of the limited dialogue of the Senecan plays a definitely artificial tone. It often seems to be a little more than a brief exhibition of virtuosity to maintain interest between the longer speeches which comprise the bulk of the text.

These longer speeches are of various sorts. The prologue, setting the tone of the play, has already been discussed. Perhaps the most striking type, aside from the prologue, is what may be called in general the messenger's speech. This was a device, in Greek tragedy, for extending the scope of the action by reporting events which took place off-stage, out of range of the audience's observation. The Greek playwright was always at pains to motivate the entrance of the messenger and so maintain the realism of the action. Seneca made extensive use of the device but, assuming his audience's familiarity with the convention, was often less careful about motivating the messenger's report. He is at great pains to make the recital an enthralling narrative, complete in itself with setting, suspense and thrilling detail, if possible culminating in a climax of horror. For almost all the messenger's speeches report scenes and incidents of horror, in the majority of the plays, the catastrophe of the drama. Under the influence of school training and the recitation, in both of which elaborate descriptions were stressed, Seneca often extended overmuch the element of setting. The fourth act of the *Thyestes* presents the most extravagant description, unique however only in its length. (641 ff.)

> Atop the citadel stands Pelops' home
> Facing the blasts of Auster, its far side
> Rears mountain high to dominate the town,
> Exposing to the fury of its kings
> The stubborn folk. Here shines a palace huge
> To enclose a multitude; its gilded beams
> Columns of mottled marble hold aloft.
> Beyond these halls exposed to public view
> Stretches the private palace and, beyond,
> A secret refuge where a secret grove
> In a deep valley hides the kingdom's heart.
> No joyous trees spread branches pruned by man
> But box and cypress, woods shrouded with gloom
> Of darkest ilex. Over all there towers
> A mighty oak that lords it o'er the grove.
> Tis here the house of Tantalus withdraws
> To seek the auspices.

This is less than half of the preliminary description which goes on to tell of the trophies of ancient cruelty hanging in the grove, only to return to the natural features.

> Here in the shade rises a gruesome spring
> To lose itself within a stagnant mere
> Like to the ugly waters of the Styx
> By which heaven swears. And here in darkest night
> Are heard the groanings of the gods of hell.
> With clashing chains the grove itself resounds
> And wailing of the dead.

At last Atreus enters with the boys bound and proceeds to the slaughter with all the forms of a sacrifice, himself the priest who wields the knife.

> Beside the altar Atreus stands and glowers
> With cruel sidelong glance, as in the wood
> By Ganges' flood a hungry tigress halts
> Between two bullocks, eager after each prize,
> Unsure which first to attack, so snaps her jaws
> At one and then the other, sharpening the more
> Her hunger. So cruel Atreus scans in doubt
> The victims twain of his accursed wrath,
> Which first to kill, which slaughter to postpone.

When Atreus has made up his mind the gruesome sequel follows with at least commendable speed. Young Thyestes is the first victim.

> Finally he plunged the sword deep in his throat
> And, as he drew it out, the corspe still stood
> Long doubtful where to fall but in the end
> Fell on his uncle. He, with replenished wrath,
> Dragged to the altar the boy Pleisthenes
> To join his brother. With the bloody blade
> He severed clean the head. The trunk collapsed;
> The head rolled off with murmuring complaint.

All that the English tragedy of blood had to do with such a model was to transfer the narrated horrors to the visible stage.

Seneca did not confine his use of the messenger's speech to the report of the climactic deed of violence nor to accounts by actual messengers. In the *Hercules on Oeta* it is Philoctetes who reports the death of Hercules. In the *Hercules* Furens, Theseus gives a long account of the capture of Cerberus, beginning in true messenger fashion: "A darkling cliff hangs over shallows vast / Whose waters dead and motionless are watched / by a grim and aged ferryman". The *Oedipus Rex* shows clearly the fascination which such narratives exercised over Seneca. Instead of following the impressive example of Sophocles who revealed through the inspired words of Tiresias the truth about Laius' death at the hands of Oedipus, Seneca makes Kreon report the seer's invocation of the dead king from the lower world to disclose the fatal facts. Some twenty lines describe the setting of the rites. (530 ff.)

> Far from the city walls there stands a grove
> Dark with thick ilex: Dirce's is the spot
> Within a well washed valley. Stately woods
> Are guarded by a cypress and an oak
> Spreading unwieldy branches dry with age.

*****

> Darkling beneath, bereft of Phoebus' light,
> The unmoving waters sense the eternal chill—
> A stagnant swamp that rims a sluggish spring.

The narrative of the actual rites is swift and vivid but it is interrupted by the irrelevant introduction of the spirits of hell which precede Laius from the realm of Dis.

> Forth in serried ranks there leaped
> Full armed the serpent host, the Dircean line
> Of brothers, harvest of the dragon's teeth:
> Baleful Erinys shrieked and Madness blind,
> Horror and all the hideous brood produced
> In the eternal darkness: Grief that tore
> Her locks, Disease with weary, sickening head.
> Old Age that hates itself, uncertain Fear
> And Pestilence, the greedy scourge of Thebes.

These are followed, by way of rhetorical contrast but without relevance to the tale, by the numerous shades who come to listen to the seer.

> Straightway like fleecy clouds they haste
> To breathe heaven's freedom. Eryx scatters not
> So many falling leaves: innumerable

They come as flowers on Hybla in the spring
When gather swarms of bees, more countless they
Than waves that shatter on the Ionian shore
Or birds in winter flying from the wrath
Of Strymon's bitter cold, cleaving the sky
To exchange the Arctic snow for the warm Nile.
So thronged the shades to hear the prophet's voice.

The whole episode occupies some 130 lines, almost an eighth of of the whole play. It is preceded (with the interposition of a chorus) by a somewhat shorter but equally unnecessary scene in which Manto and Tiresias exhibit their necromancy to Oedipus. It is obvious that the rhetorical and melodramatic elements appealed more strongly to Seneca than the strictly dramatic. If further evidence is necessary it is to be found in such a messenger's speech as that which occupies the whole of Act IV of the *Oedipus* which, with no one present to hear it, is addressed to the audience only unless we accept the unresponsive chorus as a real character.

The second type of longer speech which Seneca favored is the monologue. This unrealistic dramatic device also had its origin in Greek tragedy, especially in Euripides. But the Greek drama, with its ever-present and participating chorus, gave the semblance of realism to the monologue by furnishing at least a theoretical audience. A nurse or other confidante as the recipient of the speakers' inmost thoughts and emotions served the same purpose. Both devices were used by Seneca, but his chorus was such a shadowy and passive participant in the action as to be rarely recognisable as the recipient of the intimate addresses which became, as a result, real monologues. The same is true to a lesser degree of the confidante.

When Medea enters at the beginning of Act II with the words, "we are outdone," there is no one indicated to whom the words can be addressed. Rhetorical questions and exclamations form the bulk of this declamation which includes exhortations to herself and threats against Kreon. Only after twenty-five lines does the Nurse disclose her presence and interrupt with "Be silent, I beseech you." She herself presently soliloquises in Medea's absence (382 ff.) and, soon after, she and Medea and Jason, each ignoring the presence of the others, excitedly reveal their thoughts and plans in violent soliloquies. The *Medea* is perhaps more richly supplied with these unrealistic speeches than most of the plays, but all produce monologues. Two examples from the *Thyestes* will suffice to illustrate the monologues of Seneca. They serve to present in sharp contrast the characters of the two brothers. First, Atreus addressing himself. (176 ff).

> Coward, inert, unstrung and, worst of all
> For tyrant absolute, still unavenged,
> In face of crimes unnumbered, treacheries
> Your brother has devised, all honor breached,
> Shall Atreus' wrath be spent in useless plaints?
> All earth should now be ringing with your arms,
> The sea with clashing fleets, cities and fields
> Should be ablaze, scourged by devouring war.

*****

> Up then, my soul, perform what future time
> Shall ne'er condone, yet never shall forget.
> Dare now some impious, bloody act, the which
> Your brother well may envy, for his crimes
> Are unavenged till you surpass them all.

The victim of this hatred is depicted in what amounts to another monologue which follows at line 449. It is actually spoken to Thyestes' young son and therefore cannot strictly be called a monologue. The small boy, however, seems to be practically forgotten and the speech has all the characteristics of self-communication.

> Oh, how good
> To be a curse to none, to eat safe meals
> Stretched out on mother earth. Crimes enter not
> The humble home: the simple crust partaken
> At lowly board is taken without fear.

Poison is drunk from golden goblets. Yea,
I speak whereof I know. Ill fortune may
With reason be our choice rather than good.
The modest citizen will never shake
In terror for his home perched high in state
Upon the mountain peak. No ivory
Shines splendid in my halls, no watchman guards
My sleep; I seek no fish with argosies
Nor build stone barricades to fend the sea.

*****

I know no fear, my house is safe, unguarded,
And so great peace attends my humble state:
Tis royal power to know no need of power.

The contrast between the simple life and that in a palace of gold and ivory is familiar from the philosophy of Horace. As used here, it is typical of the mixture in Seneca's product of two dominant strains, rhetoric and Stoic Satire. They are never wholly separable and one element dear to both appears throughout the plays, in dialogue, in extended speeches and also in the choral odes and other lyric passages. This is the passion of the age for the pointed phrase whether it be in the form of a *sententia* or merely expressed in a crystalized and notable utterance. In such epigrammatic maxims the plays of Seneca abound. "Who can be forced has never learned to die." (H.F. 426.) "Men are the outcome, not the cause of war." (H.F. 407.) *Hercules Furens,* 251, has been best translated by Marston in *The Malcontent*: "Mischief that prospers men do virtue call. Behind the arrogant rides the avenging god." (Th. 614.) "Freedom so near at hand makes bold the aged." (Ph.139.) "What Reason cannot, Time has often healed." (Ag.130.) "So when you scan the gift scan too the giver." (Th.416.) These are but samplings taken at random of the sententious maxims. Some of the true *sententiae* are a familiar part of the Stoic's stock in trade: "Twas earth's first day fashioned the ultimate" (Oed.988); "So follow Nature as the guide of life: / Frequent the city and the public life" (Ph.619). Phrases like

venenum in auro bibitur (poison is drunk from golden cups)
(Th.453) were in general circulation and perhaps others are commonplace too, but some suggest a personal significance as coming
from the unhappy minister of Nero: "The blame for crime com-
pelled is his who ordered" (Tr.870); "Who profits by a crime,
the crime is his" (Med.500); "God will regard the motive pure of
sin" (Th.489).

In the majority of Seneca's *sententiae* there is a moral tone re-
sembling the maxims of Stoic Satire. The same is true of numerous
long speeches such as that of Thyestes quoted above. Such eulogies
of the simple life are reminiscent of Horace. Thyestes uses ivory
and gold to symbolize wealth as did Horace and even refers (460)
to the building operations on the shore front at Baiae which
Horace repeatedly condemned. Hippolytus, in the *Phaedra* (482
ff.) pronounces an eighty-two line Stoic sermon. He first arraigns
avarice and ambition, passing on to a scornful thrust at gold-
encrusted beams and countless columns and thence to the conventional contrast, the simple country life.

> He lords it over unspoiled country, breathes
> Untainted air in rustic innocence.
> No tricks he knows save how to snare the beasts
> In chase. When weary with long toil, he seeks
> Snowy Ilissus to restore his strength.

Again the picture swings to the reverse: the arrogant rich man
drinks from treacherous gold. But the honest peasant approaches
the life of the Golden Age when:

> The fields produced unbidden; human kind
> Contented had no fears; the woods produced
> Their simple wealth and caves their simple homes.

Then came the craving for wealth and pleasure and power; might
usurped the place of right; war followed with all its horrors until
brother turned against brother and son against father. It is an

alternating picture of virtue and vice already familiar in philosophy and poetry.

It is in the choral odes that the philosophic interest of Seneca is most conspicuous. The chorus is no longer in these plays an essential and integrated character. It has almost become a mere mechanical device for dividing the play into acts. It is therefore not surprising that the "odes" are no longer closely knit with the plot. They do in general reinforce the tone which pervades the action. Since the plays are not intended for presentation on the stage but for recitation, the choral odes are no longer associated with the dance, as in their Greek prototypes, and, as a natural result, their metrical qualities are not really choral but satiric or lyric. Horatian meters (without the nice stanzaic construction characteristic of the earlier poet) prevail but are used without discrimination and frequently in bizarre mixture. In them Seneca reverts to his early misconception of himself as a lyric poet. His facility, especially with anapests, is remarkable, but his taste is often questionable and his poetic imagination extremely limited.

The first ode of the *Hercules Furens* illustrates the pitfalls which persistently threatened the author under these circumstances. In Greek tragedy the first ode accompanied the entrance of the chorus, following the prologue. It was therefore normally in anapests, a metrical type suitable to marching. In this first ode of the *Hercules*, Seneca retains the traditional meter but the content of the ode is ideally ill-suited to accompany the march: first, a picture of dawn in the country, emphasizing the simple rustic peace of the humble; second, by way of contrast, an arraignment of the uneasy life of the wealthy; finally, an Horatian exposition of the ambitious striving of humankind contrasted with the poet's own simple and secluded life. Horace had treated the same material both semi-prosaically in the Satires and lyrically in the Odes. Seneca, with his uneasy anapests, loses both the calm force of the former and the imaginative charm of the latter.

Similar handicaps haunt the ode in the *Hercules on Oeta* which presents the same theme (644 ff.). Rendered in meter less suggestive of marching feet the familiar items of both simplicity and luxury are more acceptable.

The sod that's softer than the Tyrian couch
Brings slumber free from fear but gilded walls
And crimson trappings lead to wakeful nights.
Ah, could you see within the rich man's heart!
What secret cares his piled-up wealth creates:
Less violent the Bruttian torrent coursing
The strait neath Corus' blast. But evermore
The poor man's heart beats fearless. He may drink
From beechen cup but he can hold that cup
With hand that never trembles. What he eats
Is cheap and common but he fears no sword:
Blood is a draught that lurks in cups of gold.

One more example will be sufficient. It is from the *Thyestes* (391ff.) and definitely more lyric in tone.

Let who will in power rise
    To the perilous peak:
Me sweet quiet shall content:
    While, obscure, I seek
Restful peace, unknown to all
    May my life stream be.
So, when all my days are spent,
    From confusion free,
May I die, a peasant still.
    He fears death's grim toll
Who though known too well to all
    Knows not his own soul.

Horace's favorite theme of moderation, the golden mean, appears not infrequently in the choral lyrics. One brief example will be enough to illustrate the type. (Ag. 101 ff.).

Whom Fortune lifts to dizzy heights
    Shall fall with mightier crash.
His life endures whose modest state

> Is humble. Never rash,
> He follows still the middle way
>   Nor ever skirts the shore
>   Nor risks his skiff from sight of land,
>   Plying a prudent oar.

The inevitability of Fate alternates in the odes, as it does in Horace, with the fickleness of Fortune. In the *Phaedra* (978) Fortune rules perversely.

> For Fortune rules the affairs of humankind.
> Knowing no order, scattering with blind chance
> Her favors, kindliest ever to the worst.

In the *Oedipus*, on the contrary, Fate is omnipotent (980 ff.).

> By Fate we are compelled: yield ye to Fate.
> No anxious thought
> Can change the fabric wrought
> Upon the loom of Fate.
> All that befalls this race of mortal man
> All that we do, began
> Within the clouded past.
> For Lachesis, with hand that may not stay,
> Without regret
> Preserves the pattern set.
> As all things move in Fate's predestined way
> So earth's first revolution doomed our day.

As a Stoic philosopher Seneca was committed to the doctrine of Fate, but it was a fate controlled by the gods which he found it hard to justify and his desperation found expression when, as a poet, he could recognise the wanton play of Fortune. Both as philosopher and as poet and also as a human being placed by fortune (or fate) in a most unhappy position of constant frustration, Seneca was much preoccupied with the thought of death. It was both a promise and a threat. As his pupil on the throne escaped more and more completely from the restraint of his counsel it became increasingly a harbor of peace. In one ode in the *Troades* (321 ff.) Seneca for once speaks out with what seems to be his own personal anguish and, under the stress of emotion, almost vindicates his claim to be a lyric poet. The rhetorician and the Stoic philosopher for a moment disappear and the man who might have been emerges. It is only fair to Seneca to take our leave of him with what might well have been the envoi to his own book of life.

Is it truth or an idle tale
To frighten the timid soul
That our spirits live beyond the vale
And the grave is not the goal?
When our eyes are closed in death
And our last day's sun is set,
When we cease to draw this troublous breath
Is there no respite yet?
Or shall the torch of our funeral pyre
Blend body and soul in releasing fire?

All that the rising sun beholds
Or, sinking, sets aglow,
All that the ocean's stream enfolds
With its tides that ebb and flow,
All, all with the speed of heaven' steed
Shall Time the reaper take for his meed.

As each bright constellation
Speeds through eternal space,
As the master of all creation
Guides the centuries' mad race,
With the speed of Hecat turning
On her downward way to press,
So we seek with breathless yearning
That far goal of nothingness.

And the soul that reaches death
Is gone for eternity.
As a dying fire's vaporous breath
Or a cloud against the sky
So the soul that has ruled our life
Is gone with the speed of thought.
There is nought when death has ended strife
And death itself is nought.
Only the last line gleaming white
Of a race that is run in a single flight.

Fling off each fear, each hope forlorn
For Chaos and Time shall win
And the death that leaves the body shorn
Shall shatter the soul therein.

Where shall ye rest when life shall close?
Where the souls that are yet unborn repose.

CHAPTER SEVEN

Statius

FOR SOME REASON the age of the Flavians produced three epic writers and little else in the way of poets which has survived. Two of these sought subjects in ancient Greek mythological tradition, the third in early Roman history. Despite the fact that Domitian is said to have supported contents in poetry, the evidence would seem to confirm Tacitus in his description of the fifteen years of Domitian as years during which silence alone guaranteed survival. If not silence, then the avoidance of dangerous subjects. The first of these three epic writers to publish was Papinius Statius.

Lucan had been a man with independent means and a position of importance in the society of the court. He had also been a political partisan, a believer in the lost republic, his intransigence bolstered by his Stoic faith. Born at about the same time as Lucan though long outliving him, Statius was the product of the rhetor's school without either Lucan's social standing or his fire of conviction. Statius' father ran a school for young Romans at Naples and his son was one of his most apt pupils. In his early years he competed successfully in the poetry contests in Naples and at Alba Longa. On his father's death Statius moved to Rome where he frequently declaimed and where he also wrote pantomimes for the stage, a more profitable occupation than the writing of epic or tragedy for declamation. Juvenal's comments on this period of Statius' activities are slightly ambiguous but worth quoting for the light they throw on the career of a poet without social or political backing.

Numitor, poor he claims, has nought to give
His poet friend yet ample to endow
Quintilia or to buy a lion tamed
And feed it on an ample cache of meat.
The beast, I take it, costs him less to feed
Than what might soothe a poet's appetite.
Content with fame, Lucan may lie at ease
In sumptuous gardens but what profits fame
Serranus' or Saleius' penury
If there be nought but fame? The happy crowd
Flocks to their loved Thebaid and the voice
That charms them whensoe'er their Statius gives
Joy to the town, naming the happy day.
For he with sweetest note can charm their hearts
And rouse their deep desire as he recites.
But, having won their cheers, he'll starve unless
Paris shall buy Agave, virgin still.
For he it is who hands commissions out,
Decks the poet's fingers with the six months' rings.

Whether or not there is in these lines a covert sneer at the author of the *Thebaid* and the "virgin" (unpublished) the *Agave*, they make it clear that Statius had no generous patron nor any fortune of his own. There is no other mention of him in the Roman era. His own work gives no evidence of intimacy with the contemporaries whom he addresses and there seems to be little doubt that he was always a "professional" poet using his rhetorical training and his facility in composition to attract attention and to secure a modest livelihood.

It is, in fact, hard to discover any real personality in Statius. We should expect to find it in the collection of incidental poems which he published shortly after the appearance of his epic, the *Thebaid*, but which consisted of items many of which were written at considerably earlier dates. These poems are called *Silvae*. Each (with a few exceptions) is addressed to an individual and each is, as a rule, concerned with some particular occasion. They approximate in length the Satires of Horace and Persius with, however, a

wider range, 19 to 293 lines each. But they do not have the critical
and moralizing tone of Satire; they *do* have its miscellaneous character and some of its assumption of personal though one-sided
conversation. The writer is obviously at heart a professional rhetorician and does not expose his own character even in these personal verses. They are for the most part show pieces exhibiting in
meter the rhetorical types developed in the schools: the *descriptio*,
the *epithalamium*, the *epicedium*, and so on. Furthermore, Statius
himself insists that these poems are practically improvisations.
None of those in the first book, he asserts, took more than two
days to compose. Quintilian, in his definition of *Silvae*, gives this
as the decisive characteristic. It is not strange, therefore, that we
find little evidence of either the life or the personality of Statius in
the *Silvae*. They confirm the impression that the poet was primarily
a polished technician ready to turn his remarkable facility to any
production which might bring him to the attention of men of money
or influence. He was apparently given some slight recognition by
Domitian to whom in indirect fashion seven of the thirty-two
poems are addressed. He was invited to one court dinner and he
was given permission to deflect enough water from the public
source to supply his home in the country. It is hard to make any
estimate of his relations with the other persons addressed. The
number is small compared, for instance, with those to whom Martial sent verses and there is none of the warmth of friendly intimacy which the poems of Martial so often show. Statius was not,
it would seem, known to the substantial and serious group of
Spanish origin which composed such a large part of Martial's intimate circle.

The *Silvae* comprise five books, the last unfinished and probably
published after his death. They came out between 92 and 96 A.D.
Each book has a prose letter of dedication, a custom borrowed
from such prose treatises as those of Vitruvius and the elder Pliny.
With Statius the letter is also a table of contents. The subjects of
the poems cover a wide range: descriptions of the equestrian statue
of Domitian, the baths of Claudius Etruscus, the villa of Pollius
Felix, a wedding hymn for Stella, a thanksgiving for the recovery
of Rutilius Gallicus, condolence to Flavius Ursus on the death of a

favorite boy, birthday congratulations to Vibius Maximus and
Julius Menecrates, thanks to Domitian for an invitation to a state
dinner. The majority of the *Silvae* are in hexameters; the concluding poems of two books and the fourth of Book I are in hendecasyllables and, in addition to these departures from the normal, the
fourth book contains one poem each in hendecasyllables, Alcaics
and Sapphics. It is perhaps significant that the fifth book, published
after the poet's death, contains the three most personal of all the
Silvae, in fact the only ones apart from III.5, to his wife, which
deal with his own affairs and emotions. The rest all smack of the
professional workshop: conventional in form, exaggerated in sentiment and overloaded with learned allusion, with frequent use of
exclamation, rhetorical questions and apostrophe.

The first poem of Book I sets the standard for Statius' flattery
of the Emperor. It is not over fulsome according to the taste of the
day; it falls far short of Lucan's extravagant praise of Nero.
Thrown into the form of a rhetorical exercise in description (an
ekphrasis) it is done with technical skill and successfully conveys
its picture. The subject is the equestrian statue of Domitian just
dedicated in the forum. The opening lines, in view of the occasion,
make clear the subject.

> What mighty base is this which matches even
> Its vast colossus, dominating so
> The Latin forum? Did that godlike work
> Descend from heaven? Or did Sicilian forge
> Produce the statue, wearying the strength
> Of Sterope and Brontes? Or the hand
> Of Pallas fashion thee, Germanicus,
> As once the Rhine beheld thee, reins in hand,
> Or the astonished Dacian from his hills?
> Let ancient story sing the age-old praise
> Of that famed Trojan horse that for its frame
> Stripped Dindymus and Ida of their trees.
> *This* steed no Pergama with sundered walls
> Could have received nor in vast company
> The youths and maids of Troy have drawn it in,

> Not even great Hector or Aeneas' self.
> *That* guilty horse carried within its womb
> The savage Greeks: *this* comes commended by
> Its gentle rider. See how his features bear
> The marks of war suffused with kindly peace.

The opening is, in sound rhetorical tradition, intentionally abrupt and arresting. The classical allusions are sufficient to give a tone of cultivated learning without straining the intelligence of the listeners, for Sterope and Brontes and the Sicilian forge, as well as the Trojan horse and its origin were already familiar to the educated audience from their study of Vergil. The picture of Domitian as the purveyor of peace would not have been approved by Tacitus, but Statius as a professional poet with no political axe to grind speaks the official dogma. After the introductory lines (1–21) follows the identification of the statue's location in the forum (22–31) and a description of horse and rider (32–60). Then from the nearby Lacus Curtius rises the figure of the great martyr to greet the new arrival.

> The very guardian of the spot whose name
> The sacred waters of his lake preserve
> As now he heard the incessant hammering
> Of youthful might against the beaten bronze
> Raised from his hallowed haunt his unkempt head
> Decked with the well-earned oak. He shook in fear
> Before the mighty form and flashing light
> Of the great horse and thrice he plunged his head
> Back in the lake in terror. Presently
> Perceiving a new champion spake in joy:
> "Hail, offering of great gods and sire as well,
> Divinity to me long since. Now in my lake
> Fortunate to be worshiped, since tis given
> To know thee close at hand and to behold
> Thy glory. Mine the honor only once
> To win and save the Romulean peace:
> Thine to wage wars of Jupiter, to win

> The Battle of the Rhine and of the Mount
> So slow to yield to long extended Mars.
> Had then my country born thee thou had'st tried
> While I dared not, to plunge into the gulf,
> But Rome had held thee back with tightened rein."

This is the central panel of the poem, followed directly by an exaggerated account of the speed with which the statue was made (61–80) and by an elaborate climactic tribute to Domitian: all statues will yield obeissance to this one and from the heavens the deified ancestors of the prince will descend to do homage to him. May he remain long with us before he takes his place with them. The nicety of construction makes it hard to believe that this poem was really an improvisation.

Much of the same care for form is evidenced in the poem written for Lucan's widow Polla in celebration of Lucan's birthday. Again the central core of the poem is a quoted eulogy, this time by the muse Calliope. This is preceded by nineteen expository lines presenting the occasion.

> To Lucan's own day come ye all
> Whoe'er upon Dione's hill
> Roused in soul by the sistrum shrill
> Quaffs the stream from the pendent hoof.
> Ye who honor the gift of song,
> Thou, Arcadian, who devised
> The tuneful lyre and thou, Euhan,
> Leading in dance thy Bassarids,
> Thou Paean, ye Hyantean maids
> With joy weave fillets new
> To bind your locks; with ivy fresh
> Deck now your garments white.
> More amply flow the learned streams
> And burgeon forth the Aonian woods,
> And where it just admits the day
> With garlands green complete the shade.
> Lucan we sing—be silent all.

There follows the tale of Lucan's birth, a tribute to his birthplace, Baetica, (20–35), ending with a warning to Mantua not to
challenge the Spanish town. Then Calliope sings a prophecy of
Lucan's life, including notice of his early poems and a description
of the *Pharsalia*, all of which he will produce at an age less than
that of Vergil when he wrote the Culex. Ennius will yield the
palm to him and Lucretius, Varro and Ovid, and even the *Aeneid*
will do him reverence. Calliope promises also to sing the marriage
hymn at his perfect wedding. Then, with an abrupt break, comes
the mourning note for his untimely death.

> Oh, cruel Fates, too grimly stern,
> Oh, Fate, ne'er lengthened for the great,
> Why are the heights exposed to Chance?
> The best perversely ne'er grow old?
> The Nasamonian Thunderer
> Thus saw his son, his lightening course
> O'er East and West cut short, attain
> A tiny tomb in Babylon.
> So Thetis shuddered to behold
> Pelides struck by Pallas' hand,
> So I by Hebrus' murmuring bank
> Followed my Orpheus' singing head
> And so thou too (oh, impious act
> Of tyrant mad) condemned too soon
> To Lethe, singing still of war,
> With noble accents comforting
> The tombs of heroes, shalt be still.
> Oh, crime unique, oh impious crime!
> So spake she and with quivering quill
> Wiped lightly the fast falling tears.

Following the central core, the song of Calliope, there are two
short paragraphs. The first presents Lucan with Cato and Pompey
in heaven or in the Elyssian Fields whence, a proud shade, he can
hear the guilty being scourged and amongst them his persecutor
Nero, pale with horror and haunted by his mother's spirit. The sec-

ond is an appeal to Lucan to return and visit Polla: let there be
joy and no sorrow here to-day.

These two poems will illustrate sufficiently the *Silvae* as a whole.
All are, with few exceptions, the direct product of the school training, expert extensions of exercises set by the rhetor, now turned
out in impeccable verse without any great emotion or inspiration.
The exceptions are of considerable interest. In Book II there are
three short poems (77, 37, and 30 lines) in succession. The first
(II.3) concerns a striking plane tree at the villa of Atidius Melior.

> A tree there is that shades in close embrace
> The glittering waters of Atidius' lake,
> A tree that, bending from its lowest trunk
> Into the waters, thence, upright once more,
> Rears high its top as though reborn, the while
> Its roots draw silent nurture from the lake.
> Why turn to Phoebus to explain the cause
> So trifling? Nay, ye Naiads, (tis enough)
> And you, ye Fauns, complaisant sing the tale.

The "song" thus introduced is a "metamorphosis" after the
fashion of Ovid, telling the story of Pholoe pursued by Pan and
saved by Diana when she is changed into the plane tree on Melior's
estate. It is followed by an address to Melior which gives the occasion for the poem.

> This is the gift I bring you on the day
> That celebrates your birth: though slight the gift
> It may perchance live long. You in whose heart
> Untroubled dwell in peace Honor serene
> And Virtue gay but still impregnable;
> You who have naught to do with indolence
> Nor unjust power nor hopes incontinent,
> Whose even course lies fair midway between
> Honor and pleasure, whose integrity
> Can not be sullied, you who never knew
> The secret tumults of the heart, since all

Your life lies open to the world, who spurn
With careless scorn the lure of gold, yet know
The use of wealth not hoarded in the dark:
With such perpetual youth of mind and soul
May you surpass in years the sires of Troy,
The years too which your parents carried down
To the Elyssian Fields. Twas they who won
This boon from the grim Sisters, Blaesus too
Whose glory saved by you shall never die.

The combination of an aetiological myth with a birthday greeting does not perhaps remove the poem from the category of classroom exercise, but its comparative brevity at least suggests an expanded epigram. This quality is even more apparent in the two poems which follow. These deal with the death of a pet parrot belonging to the same Melior and the appearance of a tame lion in the arena. They are half as long as the birthday poem, almost the same length as Martial's longest epigrams. They suggest an intermediate stage between the "trifles" of Catullus and the epigrams of Martial, a stage which is perhaps best represented by the unique poem on "Sleep" (V.4).

What have I done, thou kindliest of the gods,
How sinned, poor wretch, that I alone must lose
Thy gifts, oh Sleep? The flocks are silent all,
The birds and forest beasts, even the hills
Bow as in sleep; the rushing streams have ceased
Their wonted clamor and the singing sea
Is stilled and gently laps the silent shore.
The seventh moon returns to find me snared
In sleepless suffering and the Oetaean torch
The Paphian star, have seven times visited
My couch and seven times Tithonia
Has listened to my plaints and pitying
Has sprinkled me with dewdrops from her scourge.
How can I live? I have no thousand eyes
Like cursed Argus who with changing watch

> Need never lie awake with all at once.
> But now, oh Sleep, if there be somewhere one
> Who holds his sweetheart in his loving arms
> The long night through and drives you from his couch
> Come thence to me. I do not ask to feel
> On my poor eyes the comfort infinite
> Of your spread wings: that the more fortunate
> May pray. But touch me only—tis enough—
> With your light wand or pause with bended knee
> One instant as you pass.

Here is the lyric emotion which is lacking in the more formal productions of Statius but even here the inevitable urge toward sentimentality and artificiality intrudes to betray the professional rhetorician.

During the years in which Statius produced his occasional *Silvae* he was working on a serious epic in which the same qualities of the public recitation predominate. The *Thebaid* is the story of the "Seven Against Thebes" best known to us from the play of Aeschylus. Statius has, however, introduced a vast amount of additional matter in order to extend the tale to a total of twelve books, which he took as the orthodox number set by Vergil. For there can be no doubt that to a great extent he took Vergil as his model. In the first book we find a council in heaven outlining a plan of operation, a wild storm in which Polynices and Tydeus meet and fight each other and finally at a royal banquet hero meets fatal heroine. As the epic progresses we find in the next book, Tydeus fighting against ambushed troops in a narrow gorge, in Book III a debate on "war or peace" at the court of the challenged party, and in Book IV a "catalogue" combining mythology and geography. Book VI recounts the funeral games which wind up the preamble to war. There is a lower world scene in Book VIII and in Book X a definite parallel to Vergil's incident of Nisus and Euryalus. To match the suicide of Amata in the *Aeneid,* Statius produces Iocaste (resuscitated presumably from her traditional hanging episode) to stab herself and eliminate the last element of defiance. Statius makes no effort to conceal these echoes: in fact, he winds up the adventure of Hopleus and Dymas with lines which definitely recall the Nisus and Euryalus episode.

> You too, immortalised, though verse of mine
> Rise from a lesser lyre, shall live renowned
> Down through the ages and perchance shall be
> Accepted by Euryalus to share
> His glory and the fame of Nisus' deeds.

Again and again a reasonably close quotation from Vergil acknowledges the debt of Statius.

But, while the overall plan of the *Thebaid* owes much to Vergil, the tone and spirit of the epic are totally different. What these are is indicated by the opening lines and by the prelude which they introduce.

> Fraternal battle lines and kingdoms shared
> In hate incestuous, guilt-driven Thebes,
> Pierian inspiration bids me tell.
> Whence, Goddesses, your will that I begin?
> Shall I recount the origin remote
> Of that accursed race, Sidonian rape,
> The ruthless compact of Agenor's law
> And ancient Cadmus scouring the seas?

This tone of guilt and horror is reinforced by a dozen lines in which Statius renounces the account of earlier horrors in the house of Cadmus in order to begin with Oedipus. Then, after sixteen lines of flattery addressed to the emperor, the prelude of horror is again taken up, concluding with *immodicum irae Tydea* and *alio Capaneus horrore*. It is true that Achilles' wrath and Odysseus' toils are not light-hearted subjects for the poet's lyre and that even *arma virumque* introduces a tale of hardship. But these all have the heroic element, the promise of high adventure. Even the ominous opening of the *Pharsalia* with its *bella plus quam civilia* does not have the same effect though it is not at first easy to say just why. Both poets call upon their greatest powers of artificial usage,

employing the rhetorical question and exclamation. Statius surely
had Lucan in mind when he chose *fraternas acies* as his first two
words and wrote into the context his dedication to Domitian in a
fashion not unlike that in which Lucan introduced his even more
fulsome flattery of Nero. But Lucan deals with understandable
human horrors, the civil wars of a recent century. Statius adds to
the horror of fraternal contests the terror of the supernatural, the
curse of god and the fabulous guilt and imprecations of Oedipus.
This is the tone of the prologue of a Senecan tragedy and it is used
for the same purpose.

Herein lies a real distinction between the epics which we are
discussing. For Vergil the motivating inspiration had been patriotic
pride in the achievement of Rome. Arms, the hero and Rome set
the key. Toils are implied but they are the toils which lead to great
results. Lucan too had Rome in mind but it was a lost Rome and
the battles were from his point of view disastrous losses for both
sides. Such heroism as the *Pharsalia* presents is the dogged courage
of Stoic martyrdom. Vergil is the complete artist with his heart set
not on the reaction of his audience but on the perfection of his
work. Lucan is an artist too but a self-conscious artist who would
step to the guillotine with an epigram on his lips. Statius is again
different. He is not interested in a great artistic masterpiece nor in
the memorial of a lost cause. He is the actor in a melodrama intended to tingle the nerves of the audience with a continuous
series of gruesome thrills. In the *Thebaid* we come as close to pure
rhetorical epic as we do to pure rhetorical tragedy in the *Thyestes*
of Seneca. Even a step closer, because Seneca never escaped the
grip of Stoic Satire and Statius did.

The parallel with the tragedy is made more obvious once the
theme has been stated. For, like the motivating ghost, Oedipus
appears with an introduction every word of which is selected to
add to the tone of horror. His curse sends Tisiphone forth to loose
the deadly strife which is to be the play. The prologue is complete.
Action starts with the fatal decision at Thebes to divide the rule.

In these first 200 lines nearly all of the characteristics of Statius'
art appear. Enough has been said perhaps about the pervading
sense of horror but it should be noted that this is scarcely relaxed

throughout the poem. Some of its force is possibly lost by the characteristic intrusion of Oedipus' whole life history into his invocation of Tisiphone, but the purpose of this somewhat unnatural intrusion is to add further horrors even if they are not wholly relevant. And it would not be in character for Statius to overlook a chance to bring in, if possible allusively, the knowledge which he has accumulated to impress his audience. The Thebans are "Echionian folk" and their land "Ogygian." Cadmus is referred to as "searching the Carpathian Sea for the fair burden of the bull" until as an exile he came to "the Hyantean Fields where in the furrows of the fertile earth he sowed fraternal strife." The hissing of Tisiphone's snaky locks is heard not only by all the shore of the Achaean Sea but by Parnassus and Eurotas; Oeta was rocked by it and the Isthmus was almost wiped out; his mother seized Palaemon from his dolphin and pressed him to her breast. None of this geographical and mythological lore is particularly recondite but it is obtrusive and unnecessary and lends itself to both exaggeration and to obscurity. The last item adds a typically irrelevant bit intended to add to the grim terror by the contrasted touch of sentimentality. Even in this short section there is much more of this learned allusion, enough to burden the reader: it could hardly more than dazzle the hearer at the recitation—certainly it did not help his understanding. It would take a listener of quick reaction and considerable miscellaneous information to catch at first hearing the meaning of the light in Tisiphone's eyes: *sedet intus abactis / ferrea lux occulis, qualis per nubila Phoebes / Atracia rubet arte labor.*

The reminiscence of Lucan's *Pharsalia* in the opening words of the *Thebaid* has already been noted but the borrowing is more extended. At line 125 there begins a series of qualities and emotions, sharply defined, clearly stated, for the most part abstract, epigrammatically presented. This is not Statius' style, and it at once recalls the opening of the *Pharsalia* (1. 128). With *iurisque secundi ambitus impatiens,* the recollection becomes specific. Lucan's *impatiensque loci fortuna secundi* (1. 124) springs to mind, the parallel confirmed by the *stare loco* which begins line 130. In an attempt to vary the conclusion of this section Statius replaces

Lucan's *exiguum dominos commisit asylum* with the less epigrammatic *pugna est de paupere regno*. But this very departure from his usual practice, this creation of the pointed phrase, calls attention to the slight impropriety of the lines to which it forms the conclusion. To Lucan, dealing with Roman history, the traditional hatred of brothers toward each other naturally recalled Romulus and Remus and the contrast of what they fought over with the luxurious and powerful Rome of a later day was a natural afterthought. Statius tries to draw a similar contrast at Thebes but falls at once into the pitfall offered by a familiar Roman commonplace. The phrase *crasso laquearia fulva metallo* betrays him. This is a stock characterization of Roman luxury, a part of the armory of Satiric weapons. With this familiar commonplace the epigrammatic conclusion is wholly in character but the whole is a purple patch for Statius rather foreign to his usual manner.

Fundamental in all of this is the self-conscious attitude of the recitation artist. The traditional epic was an objective tale told for its inherent interest as a story. Homer was satisfied with one personal word addressed to the Muse: "Sing, Muse, Achilles' wrath" and Vergil, though he added the personal *mihi*, was equally objective: "Sing to me Muse the cause, what god's despite." But Vergil made a slight concession to the neoteric poets of personal verse: "*I* sing of arms and of the man who came / First from the shores of Troy to Italy, / Exiled by fate, unto Lavinia's strand." He also used the word "causes" making clear however that these were concrete and not abstract economic causes: "There was an ancient city: men of Tyre", etc. Lucan expanded his causes at great length into a dissertation on the moral and economic reasons for civil war. He did not intrude personally into his long prologue but he made it a presentation of personal belief and prejudice. Statius steps forward as the recitation artist, speaking in his own person to win the interest of his audience, discarding (with a considerable show of learning) numerous possible points of departure and then expanding the causes for the doom of Thebes.

This personal intrusion of the poet is flagrantly obvious in the concluding lines of the epic. (XII.797–819).

I could not, though some god should give my heart
The outlet of a hundred tongues, aspire
To tell in worthy lines the funeral pyres
Of commoners and leaders mingled there
With groans confused, nor how, from frenzy bold,
Evadne seized the fires that held her love
And summoned to her heart the thunderbolt;
How Tydeus' tortured wife, prone to embrace
His savage body, sprang to his defence;
Or how Argia to her sister told
Her cruel watch; how Erymanthia mourned
With clamorous wailing for her Arcas slain,
Arcas whose manly face was calm in death.
Arcas bewailed alike by armies twain.
Fresh inspiration or Apollo's self
Could naught avail: my barque, its journey done,
O'er endless seas has won at last to port.
    Wilt thou survive the years and still be read
Your master gone, Thebaid mine, that now,
For twice six years my unremitting care,
Hast kept me sleepless? Fortune has surely spread
A kindly way before you and begins
To make your future. Caesar with generous heart
Has deigned to know you and the youth of Rome
Study you and commit to memory
Your lines. Live on, I pray. But challenge not
Vergil's divine Aeneid: reverently
Follow its footsteps. Then, if jealousy
Still clouds thy glory, it will disappear:
When I am gone shall come the praise I've earned.

These two characteristics, the self-conscious presence of the narrator and the tone of melodramatic horror, pervade the entire epic. Oedipus invokes Tisiphone at the beginning and she makes several appearances to spur on horrors: ghosts (both Laius and Amphiaraus) and omens and the ever intervening gods serve also to

maintain the atmosphere of melodrama. From the first incidents of
the story, the fight between Polynices and Tydeus, in a fiercely
raging storm before the palace of Adrastus, through the drought
which tortures the Argive army on its way to Thebes, the earth-
quake which swallows up Amphiaraus, the first skirmish before
Thebes, the laments of Antigone and Ismene, the successive deaths
of the heroes culminating in the mutual destruction of Eteocles and
Polynices, Oedipus' lament, Iocaste's suicide, Antigone's exile, the
weight of horror is rarely lifted. Even the final arrival of the chival-
rous Theseus is overshadowed by the mourning over the Athenian
dead which concludes the poem.

If we may judge from the other narrative poems of the period
and by the plays of Seneca, this inspiring of terror in the audience
was popular with those who attended the recitations. Of the epic
writers, Statius outdoes the rest. But he was also master of the
descriptive passage and his brilliant descriptions serve to relieve
the monotony of horror. He applies his virtuosity to the description of persons (eleven lines are given to Tisiphone at her first
appearance), to places (the most famous is that of the Grove of
Sleep in X.84–117), to scenes of necromancy, to battlefields and
to funeral games. Nevertheless, except insofar as he stops to ex-
aggerate the tone of horror, his descriptions cannot be said seriously to delay his story. They are sometimes too much extended
and too dependent on a cumulative effect. Statius does not have
Vergil's touch for finding the exact phrase but, on the other hand,
his descriptions do not impede the narrative or stand as independent units as much as do those of Lucan. The same is true of
his learning and literary information. Lucan might pause for long
periods to produce masses of information about witchcraft or serpents. Statius introduces the products of his research both by allusion and by direct statement but always in the course of the
narrative, not in independent paragraphs. He is also unexpectedly
sparing of *sententiae*. He did, however, introduce digressions in the
form of largely irrelevant stories brought in for their own inherent
interest. The longest is that of Hipsypyle, told by herself (V.17–
498), but there are also Admetus' story of Apollo and Coroebus

(I.557–661), the fatal necklace of Hermione (II.268–305), and the tale of Hopleus and Dymas (X.347–448).

Both Lucan and Statius derived admittedly from Vergil but they represent two different possibilities in the rehandling of Vergil's epic art. Both men were poets by the gift of nature. This does not mean that they were of the greatest, the truly inspired poets, but their command of the verse medium and their facility in its use justify the statement. Lucan was a man involved by the conditions of birth and environment and by his own nature, however volatile, in the affairs of Rome's ruling class. Furthermore, he was so fiercely a part of the conservative group within that class as to have an iron bound point of view which controlled throughout his attitude toward his characters and his work. Statius, with no such preconditioning, was the son of a successful "grammaticus", uninhibited by his environment, with no greater motive than the will to succeed with the only audience which he knew, the supporters of the declamatory soirees. Both had the conventional training in the schools but to Lucan the fruit of this training was a means to an end, to Statius it was an end in itself. They both sought their ends by means of poetry but along totally different lines. Lucan, with all the earnestness of an opposition orator, used the school training to present a cause, the desperate cause of Stoic opposition. Statius had none of this desperate earnestness: he used the tools which the school training put in his hands to make a demonstration of his masterly skill in their manipulation. In the product of the one we have, as Quintilian clearly saw, the work of a poet-orator, persuading his readers with every means at his command; in the output of the other, a form of art for art's sake. Each created an epic which lacked unity because, for different reasons, their hearts were in the perfection of the parts rather than the whole. Each used the popular arts of description and exaggeration, of tantalizing allusion and impressive display of learning. But the Satiric earnestness and moral criticism, so prominent in Lucan, is almost entirely absent from the poem of Statius. The latter could and did draw on the former but not to the end of overall imitation. The horrors of Lucan are often as grotesque as those of Statius but they are not presented wholly for their own sake even though the poet is often carried away by his own artistry and exaggerates them outrageously. They at least leave the impression of having been introduced for an ulterior purpose which is not true of those of Statius.

From a critical point of view, the important fact is that both poets tended to make the epic more episodic and less dramatic. Both contributed to the tendency to move from the heroic epic toward the more melodramatic, working on the more temporary and superficial emotions rather than on the larger and deeper, more universal and enduring human reactions.

Unfortunately for Statius' reputation there have survived something over a thousand lines of another epic, the *Achilleid*. Whether the rest of the poem has been lost or was never written we have no way of knowing. What we have of it confirms all that has been said about the *Thebaid* most emphatically. A literal translation of the opening lines will indicate the allusive obscurity of the style. "Of great hearted Aeacides and the offspring feared by the Thunderer and forbidden to inherit his father's heaven, relate, goddess." Aeacus was the grandfather of Achilles; the Thunderer, of course, is Zeus; Zeus, warned that the child of Thetis would be greater than his father, yielded Thetis to Peleus. (Compare with this Homer's beginning of Achilles' story: "Sing, goddess, the wrath of Peleus' son Achilles.") The remaining eleven lines of the prelude are concerned chiefly with the poet himself, for, after stating that he intends to tell the whole story of Achilles' life, not merely the part contained in the *Iliad*, he recalls with pride (or, perhaps better, with unbounded conceit) his own authorship of the *Thebaid*. "Thebes numbers me with her forefathers and with her own Amphion." This is followed by six lines of flattering dedication to Domitian.

It might be expected that, with the opening of the narrative, Statius' style might become more succinct and clear, but such is not the case. "The Dardan shepherd had loosed his fleet from the Oebalian shore having nonchalantly laid waste careless Amyclae and fully carrying out the portent of his mother's dream and was retracing his guilty passage where Helle, now a Nereid, deep buried in the sea, rules over the hated waves, when Thetis—alas, never in vain the premonitions of parents—took fright beneath the glassy surge at the Idaean oars. With no delay she burst forth from her watery couch accompanied by her throng of sisters: the narrowing shores of Phrixus swarm and the narrow water does not accommodate its mistresses." All of which means that Paris, whose mother Hecuba had dreamed that she was giving birth to a fire-brand, had set out from Sparta on his way back to Troy and had reached the Hellespont when Thetis, alarmed at the sound of oars, rose from the depths with the other Nereids to see what was happening. These ten lines of narrative are immediately followed by twenty lines of soliloquy on the part of Thetis. The opportune appearance of Neptune—it takes ten lines to picture his spectacular arrival—gives rise to speeches of sixteen and fifteen lines by Thetis and Neptune. It is unnecessary to follow in detail the whole story of the book which proceeds in the same fashion through the account of the concealment of Achilles disguised as a girl by his mother on the island of Scyros, his discovery by Ulysses and Diomede and his departure with them for Troy. Perhaps the best portion is Achilles' own story of his early training by Chiron told on shipboard to his deliverers.

> Scarce had my young life passed the span
> Of twice six revolutions of the year
> Before he made me overtake in speed
> Swift stags and Lapith steeds, on foot to pass
> The weapon that he threw. And often too
> Chiron himself, while still his years allowed,
> Chased me at headlong speed across the plains.
> And when the wild course through the meadow land
> Left me exhausted he would laugh with joy
> And lift me to his back.

If Statius could have restrained his passion for decoration and written always in this simpler narrative style he might have composed great epics instead of the rhetorical failures which he did produce.

CHAPTER EIGHT

Valerius Flaccus

OF THE LIFE of Valerius, or to give him his full name, Valerius Flaccus Setinus Balbus, very little is known, not even his place of birth. In his epic, the *Argonautica*, in addressing Vespasian he mentions the capture of Jerusalem (70 A.D.) by Titus (not yet emperor) and Quintilian, writing after 92 A.D., speaks of his recent death. The *Argonautica* must therefore have been composed between 70 and 91. Valerius' life span may be placed conjecturally at 50 to 91.

Lucan, at mid-century, had shown what the rhetorical training when transferred from oratory to poetry could do for the historical epic. He was wholly representative of the Age of Rhetoric and Satire. Statius, the professional rhetor, had attempted with less success to do the same for the mythological epic. His product lacked the drive which Stoic conviction and satiric bitterness gave to the *Pharsalia*. The *Thebaid*, rich in melodramatic incident, exhibited all the devices of the school but almost none of the influences of Stoic satire. Valerius, Statius' contemporary, chose also to write mythological epic and selected a far more appealing subject than that of the Theban cycle. The tale of the Argonauts and their voyage to recover the Golden Fleece was full of romantic incident, requiring less support from rhetoric to maintain audience appeal, and Valerius, with no apparent interest in contemporary politics or the social evils of his day, had no recourse to Stoic satire. He was master of all the rhetorical devices but concealed them with greater skill than did the orator Lucan or the professional rhetor Statius.

Both Lucan and Statius, deficient in dramatic sense, lacked a

hero. And so, at the start, it would seem did Valerius. His opening
lines, Like Lucan's, envision incidents but not a hero.

> I sing of conquest o'er the primeval sea
> By mighty sons of gods, of that famed ship
> That ventured to assail the farthest shore
> Of Scythian Phasis, burst a passage through
> The Clashing Rocks, at least to rest in peace
> On bright Olympus.

And, true to that promise, the trip of the Argonauts to Colchis
consists of a series of incidents, citing the ports touched at with
such adventures as took place at each. The gods are constantly in
evidence as a motivating influence, for Valerius could hardly exclude them from a mythological epic as Lucan had from his historical poem. The practical human incentive to the Argonautic trip
is provided by Pelias the old Thessalian king who is fearful of
Jason as a threat to his power. Curiously enough Valerius does not
tell of the oracle that caused Pelias' fear, that of the man coming
with one sandal, but simply states that Pelias feared the valor and
repute of Jason and so sent him off to meet his death in the hopeless quest of the Golden Fleece. Athena furnishes the ship and
Juno prepares the way for the heroes. Then follows the launching
of the Argo, the gathering of the heroes and (on their departure)
the catalogue of their names. While they are riding out a great
storm (reminiscent of Vergil) Pelias, further to assure his own
safety, slays Jason's father Aeson, his wife and young child. So
ends Book I.

Then begins in earnest the list of places and incidents: Pelion,
Sciathos, Sepias, Ossa, Pallene, Lemnos.

> Pelion now sinks low, plunging its lofty
> Ash trees into the sea, now disappear
> Diana's Tisian shrines. Sciathos fades
> And outstretched Sepias. Magne's fertile fields
> Disclose its pasturing horses. Now appear
> Dolope's mounds and Amyros emptying

Into the curving shore; with failing breeze
They furl the sails, bend to the oars and reach
Eurymenae. Again the breeze invites
The sail and to the straining Grecian eyes
Mist shrouded Ossa shows. Pallene next . . .

*   *   *   *   *

And now above the sea's bright surface rears
Vulcanian Lemnos, mourned for thy many toils
By thee, the god of fire; the women's rage
And crimes repel thee not; thou dost not blush
To call to mind their former kindnesses.

Then follows the story of the women of Lemnos, their slaying
of the men, the deed of Hypsipole who saved her father, the wel-
coming of the Argonauts, Jason's affair with Hypsipyle and the
departure of the Argonauts. It is Valerius' longest and most elaborate digression—if it be called a digression. It is carefully motivated in Vergilian manner: the wrath of Venus, her despatch of
Rumor and the rousing of the women. The whole story is an
epyllion with Catullan as well as Vergilian reminiscences.

The listening of sites passed is briefly resumed with Electria,
Imbros and Sigeum. There it is relieved by another romantic incident. Heracles and Telamon wander off together and come upon
Hesione, chained to a rock and threatened by a great sea monster.
She is the daughter of Laomedon who has chained her there to
avert a pestilence sent by the gods. Heracles slays the monster,
goes to Troy and demands as reward the horses given to Laomedon
by Zeus. Laomedon seeks instead to retain Heracles by a ruse in
order to kill him. Heracles threatens to return and take vengeance.
The sequel is not recounted but only hinted at. This is again not a
digression, only an expanded romantic incident.

After another list of sites—Ilium, Ida, the Dardenelles, Atlas,
Pityas, Lampsacus, Cyzicus—more than half of Book III is occupied by the war of the Argonauts with the Bebrycians. The battle
won, they cruise along the coast of Mysia. Then Heracles goes
ashore and with him Hylas. The story of Hylas, lured by the

nymphs into the spring, follows at considerable length. The Argonauts, impatient as they wait for Heracles, argue at length and
finally sail on. But the gigantic king of the Bebrycians, Amycus,
appears challenging them to send one of their number to box with
him. Pollux outwits and slays him.

As the Argonauts skirt the shore of the Bosporus the poet is
quite naturally reminded of Io, who, in her wide wanderings as a
heifer, swam across that body of water. Orpheus sings the song
of Io's wanderings to the enthralled Argonauts. Almost immediately they discover Phineus and for him they drive away the
Harpies. In return he foretells their adventures to come and gives
them instructions for getting through the Symplegades or Clashing
Rocks.

This is their next adventure, vividly related, and so they come to
Pontus on the shore of the Euxine, pass Cytorus, Carambis,
Sinope, the land of the Chalybes and Phasis and so reach Colchis.
This is of course the climax of the trip and at this point Valerius
(like Vergil) makes a new start. This time he calls on the Muse.

> Begin for me, oh Goddess, other songs
> And tell of wars which you beheld, waged by
> The great Thessalian hero. Neither my mind
> Nor yet my voice avails me for this task.

And this time the central figure is the Thessalian hero, not the
Argonauts as a group.

The meeting of the hero and heroine is dramatic. Medea has
been having a bad dream and in the morning goes out with her
attendants to purify herself in the river Phasis. On the way they
meet the group from the Argo heading for the palace under the
lead of Jason.

> The queen, though terror stole away her voice
> And left her silent, marvelled none the less
> At him, the leader: even so did he,
> Transfixed, see only her among the throng
> Of all that galaxy. He spake: "If thou

Art goddess born, the glory bright of high
Olympus, then I vow those are the orbs
Of virgin Dian, this her countenance,
And thou at peace without thy weapons dire
Art being led by these Caucasian nymphs
Unto their river haunts. But if thy home
Is in this land and thou art sprung from here,
Happy thy sire and happier still will be
The man that makes thee his in years to come.
But help, Oh Queen, us mortals. We are youths
Who come in all good will, leaders of Greece,
Seeking thy city. Lead us I pray unto
Whoever is thy king and tell me when
And how we should approach. For God indeed
Has sent you to me in my ignorance.
To your hands I entrust my very fate."
He spoke and stood facing the startled girl.
She hesitated, held a while by maiden fear,
Then spake in turn: "Aeetes whom you seek,
He is my father and our walls are near
If you choose well your way between two paths.
Follow this path: the other leads to strong
Encampments of an impious enemy."

Following Medea's directions Jason and his group reach the
palace and gaze in wonder at the great doors decorated with scenes
from the history of Colchis and (most surprising) with the arrival
and future fate of the Argonauts themselves.

Besides, with art phophetic, Mulciber
Had wrought a golden fleece and pictured there
The Greeks to come. The Pagasaean pine
Is felled by Athena's axe and she herself
Shapes oars and she, beneath the keel,
With bared right arm conducts the ordered ranks.
The south wind rises and o'er all the deep
One ship sails. Dolphins raise Odrysian song.

Then there are shown the frightened Colchians
Around the mouth of Phasis and the queen
Who leaves her father shouting after her.
There stood a city washed by twofold seas
Where sport and song prevail and in the night
The wedding torches gleam. On royal bed
The happy groom deserts his former love.
The avenging Furies watch from the roof o'erhead.
The wife displaced by mistress now prepares
A fatal gift, the product of her skill:
A poisoned veil and jewel studded crown.
Adorned with these the unhappy mistress goes
Unto her father's altar where, consumed
In flaming fire, she involves the paternal home
In mighty conflagration.

Admitted to audience by Aeetes, Jason explains his mission and
the King finally agrees to give him the Fleece if he will help conquer Perses who is in revolt with forces superior to those of Aeetes.
Jason agrees and the Argonauts perform great deeds of valor, especially Jason whom Medea watches from the wall.

But lo Medea from her father's wall
Where she was seated watched the various struggles
Of the great battle, in the dust of war
Recognized some great kings herself and learned
From Juno others—then beheld the Ausonian
Hero far off and fixed on him her eyes
And all her senses with her yearning heart:
Where now he rushed, where now he turned aside
Anticipating with her glance how many horse,
How many men he slew, stopping the stragglers
With shaft on shaft. And wheresoe'er she turned
Her wandering glance to seek her brother's deeds
Or her betrothed's, 'twas always Jason met
Her anguished search. Then with these words she spake
Her sister, feigning ignorance: "Who, pray,

Is he that I behold through all the field
Of battle raging, whom you too must see?"
And Juno answered with deep-goading guile:
"Tis Aeson's son himself you see, my sister,
Who, sailing many seas, is come to fetch
The Fleece of Phrixus (his own kinsman, he)
And none surpasses him in rank or blood.
You see how brilliantly he flashes there
Over the Minyae and the Cytaean lords,
What heaps of slain he rears. And now he'll set
His sails and leave our shores to seek the wealth
Of happy Thessaly and Phrixus' fields.
So let him go—pray god he win through all."
So much she spake and bade her more intently,
While still she may, behold the hero's deeds.

Aeetes proves false to his promises and, refusing to surrender
the Fleece, makes new conditions. Jason must yoke the great fire-
breathing bulls of Aeetes, with them plow furrows and sow in these
what are left of Cadmus' dragon teeth and then conquer the giants
that spring from these teeth. Jason, in high dudgeon, accepts the
challenge to the horror of Medea who has been listening. She re-
tires and, spurred on by Juno and Minerva, prepares her most
potent poisons. With these she secretly leaves the palace gates and
again meets Jason. After a long passage of lovemaking she gives
Jason the poison which will make his armor invulnerable. He proceeds to yoke the bulls, sow the dragon's teeth and then, as in-
structed by Medea, throws the helmet which she has given him
among the earth-born giants who proceed to fight and kill each
other. Then Medea with her drugs puts to sleep the dragon that
guards the Fleece. Jason takes the Fleece and, with it and Medea,
returns to his companions. They receive Medea gladly. Erginus
recalls to the Argonauts the difficulties of the outward journey and
suggests a new way home—up the Danube. They agree and back
they go along the Scythian coast, past Corambis and on to the
island of Peuce.

There Jason and Medea are married with the approval of all the

Argonauts except Mopsus who foresees a short-lived happiness and prays that Medea may have no children. Shortly after the marriage, Absyrtus arrives with a Colchian fleet. The inconsistent Argonauts wish to give back Medea and go home with the Fleece. And so, with Medeas' plea to Jason and one line of his response, we come to the end of the incomplete epic.

> Distraught by sudden anger, she acts first
> And, drawing aside the son of Aeson, speaks:
> "Me too, my husband, me no less than you
> These noble Grecian youth deeply concern
> By night and day. Yet I may counsel too
> (If I be not a prisoner on this ship
> Of Peleus and deceived by treachery
> Follow my captors) and should rightly know
> Your plans. I fear not, my most faithful lord,
> For my own self. Yet pity me and keep
> Your promises of wedlock till at least
> We reach Thessalia's harbor—scorn me there,
> If scorn you will, in your own home. Yourself,
> Not your companions, sware to me. For them
> 'Twere right to give me back but that same right
> Is not bestowed on you. For I shall drag you down
> To ruin with myself—not me alone,
> A guilty maid, does Colchis now seek back:
> We all aboard this ship are fugitives.
> Fear you my brother's might, my father's ships?
> Am I not worth some risk? Have I not earned
> Your comrades' deaths—your own? I would to god
> The ship had come under some other lord.
> But now let them return. They have the power
> To give me back. But you at least give ear
> To my advice: heed not too much their fears.
> Who then dared yoke the fiery bulls, who then
> Dared penetrate the dreadful dragon's den?
> Oh would to god my heart did not dare all
> For you and that my love knew some restraint!

> But look you now, you that were once so just
> And noble, were it right for me to beg
> With suppliant words? My sire thinks not so
> Nor yet that I should suffer punishment
> For crime or brook a master."

She breaks off and goes into a fury of uncontrolled ravings, goading Jason to speech. We have but one line of his answer: "Dost think that I'm afraid, could wish such things?" and our sad answer must be—yes.

The usual explanation given for this abrupt ending with the poem left incomplete is that Valerius must have died before finishing the work. This is hardly credible. The epic was begun shortly after 70 A.D. and Valerius did not die until after 90 A.D. Twenty years is too long a period for composing less than six thousand lines. It is much more reasonable to conclude that the problem of *how* to finish the epic proved too much for the poet.

Valerius had already indicated (in the prophetic decorations of the palace doors) that Medea's spectacular crimes at Corinth and her departure in the chariot of the sun were to be the climax of his tale. This he had further indicated in a prophecy of Mopsus made at the beginning of the voyage.

> What sight do I behold? Lo, Neptune calls
> A mighty council of the ocean gods
> Who loudly bid him guard his wide domain.
> Now, Juno, hold your brother with your arms:
> Desert not, Pallas, this our ship: deflect
> Your uncle's wrath. They cease and suffer now
> One ship upon the deep. But through what dangers
> Do I speed on? Why now does Hylas fair
> Suddenly hide his locks among the reeds?
> What means that urn and those caerulean robes
> On his white limbs? Whence, Pollux, come those wounds?
> And oh, what fiery breath from nostrils wide
> Of mighty bulls. From every furrow rise
> Helmets and spears and shoulders following.

What war I see around the Golden Fleece!
Who is it that I see piercing the skies
With winged serpents and her hands a-drip
With blood? Who are they whom she slays with sword?
Thou wretched son of Aeson, save thy sons
So young. I see a marriage couch in flames.

All the other events prophesied take place in what we have of
the epic so that it can hardly be questioned that this final catastrophe is what Valerius intended at the moment as the final act of his
story. But this was all before he had begun to build up Jason as a
hero and such an end would not be that of a hero. But also if he
made Jason abandon Medea at Peuce that too would be unheroic.
Furthermore Jason's return to find his father dead and Pelias still
alive and in a position to make further plots against him would be
a poor climax.

This problem involves also the question of Valerius' use of his
sources. There is no doubt that for the trip as far as Colchis he
followed the Greek epic of Apollonius of Rhodes. Apollonius, a
third century (B.C.) Alexandrian, was a rebel against the extreme
practices of his contemporaries. To him it seemed still possible to
write successfully a long epic rather than to yield weakly to the
dictum of the great Callimachus that a big book is a big evil. His
quarrel with the librarian caused his move to Rhodes whence he
is familiarly known as Apollonius of Rhodes. The epic was the
Argonautica in four long books. In spite of his insistence that he is
writing a "plain tale" his Hellenistic training is obvious in his development of local traditions, local geography and dramatic situa-
tions. His brilliant treatment of the love affair of Jason and Medea
overshadowed his weakness in dealing with the voyage out to
Colchis and back and probably exercised a real influence on the
Aeneas-Dido incident of Vergil's *Aeneid*. Valerius follows fairly
closely (with improvements of his own) the story as presented by
Apollonius up to the time of Jason's arrival at Colchis.

It is at this point that Valerius makes his new invocation so
reminiscent of Vergil. Medea then guides Jason as Venus in dis-
guise guided Aeneas. Juno wraps Jason in a cloud (again a remi-

niscence of the *Aeneid* but this time with no sound motivation) and the decorations of the palace doors inevitably recall Dido's palace. The story from here on diverges widely from Apollonius. But, while he seems from this point to have had Vergil's *Aeneid* in mind, Valerius had neither the material nor the ability to rival his model. Vergil had made his foreign enchantress powerful by her human qualities, by no means uncivilised, magnificent but wholly human. She was for the hero Aeneas not a savior, the solution of his problem, but his greatest and final temptation to abandon his mission for an easier and alluring solution.

It is then a reasonable suspicion that the difficulties of the situation, moral and physical, are what really account for the incompleteness of the poem, that Valerius never worked out a solution of his dilemma. A poet of the recitation school, he would have found no difficulty in creating sufficient incidents to satisfy his audience but he had reached a point where he may well have despaired of making some sort of consistent character out of the conflicting fragments of hero which he had already assembled.

This central difficulty is typical of Valerius' failure as a poet. For, in spite of being completely master of the epic verse and in spite of having an exciting story to tell, it cannot be denied that Valerius very quickly palls. He made little impression on his contemporaries and even less on posterity. Lacking both the inspiration of a genius and the power of a denouncing prophet, he left to the world an unfinished failure as the best evidence that, while rhetoric and Stoic satire might enrich certain fields of literature, indeed might inspire a Lucan to unique individual success, they had not enriched but, to a large degree, put an end to the tradition of the Roman epic.

CHAPTER NINE

Silius Italicus

To some extent the extravagance of the Age of Rhetoric and Satire had been curbed before Silius Italicus wrote his seventeen-book epic on the wars of Rome and Carthage. Statius' *Thebaid,* while it had been definitely a product of the Rhetor's school, had abandoned the field of contemporary history and the patriotic tone of Stoic satire. Valerius had reacted still further from the popular recitation manner and had shown a tendency to revert to the Vergilian model in the framework of his romantic epic but without the fervor of national pride. He also jettisoned the satiric adherence to Stoic morality.

Caution is necessary in estimating any such apparent change or in extending it beyond the range of personal motive. The writers whose work has survived from the Age of Nero were all men definitely opposed to the regime in power. This was about the only personal characteristic which they had in common. Persius, the earnest preacher of Stoic decency, Lucan, the high-strung poet, out of favor with the emperor, and Seneca, the disappointed statesman, insecure and resentful, all reacted strongly against the centralized power of Nero and his alien intimates and against the profligate cheapness of the new aristocracy. Their weapons were the school rhetoric and the Stoic satire. By the time of Domitian, Statius and Valerius Flaccus had no political axes to grind. Their education was the same as that of Lucan but they were no longer concerned with moral or governmental questions and their products show little of the old Stoic violence: only the proverbial Stoic clichés remain. Silius Italicus was for a time concerned with politics but not in opposition to the emperor and not in a very serious way and he had definitely retired. Stoicism was a religion wtih him, not a weapon of attack. He seems to have withdrawn from politics without resentment and turned wholeheartedly to poetry. In this field it is clear that he was at heart more reactionary than either of his contemporary poets. Silius' epic is a deliberate return to the poetry of national glorification without the intrusion of personal ambition to win rhetorical honors. As will appear, however, the genius of this patriotic aristocrat was not strong enough to withstand altogether the influences of which he disapproved.

Unlike his contemporaries who wrote epic poetry Silius was a man of importance in the state. The last consul under Nero (68 A.D.), proconsul of Asia under Vespasian, he passed the rest of his life in the cultivated leisure of a distinguished man of wealth and influence with a deep devotion to literature and to the great men of letters of the past. His estates embraced the site of Vergil's tomb and one of Cicero's villas. Pliny wrote to his friend Caninius Rufus about Silius on the occasion of his death at the age of seventy-five. After explaining the poet's Stoic suicide, the result of incurable cancer, he gives a clear picture of Silius' dignified retirement, occupied with his literary creativity and surrounded by important friends, *sine potentia, sine invidia.* Pliny cannot refrain from suggesting that Silius had injured his reputation under Nero by "voluntary legal attacks" but adds that by his praiseworthy use of leisure he had "wiped out the stain of his busyness." Martial's tribute to Silius (IV.14) accompanying the gift of a volume of his poems is equally revealing, slightly warmer in tone and, it seems to me, wholly sincere.

> Silius, glory of the sisters nine,
> Who dost in mighty tomes conquer again
> The perjuries of Carthage, all the wiles
> Of Hannibal, and force his fickle folk
> To yield before the Scipionic might,
> One moment put aside thy sterner stuff,
> Now when the merry month of Saturn rings
> With sportive gaming: mid the rattling dice
> Bestow thy leisure on my lighter verse.

Nor read with scowling brow but smile a bit
At these bold tablets dripping wantonness.
So once I ween Catullus might have dared
Commit his Sparrow to great Maro's hand.

Pliny was less enthusiastic about the product of Silius' pen than
was Martial. "He wrote," says Pliny, "with more pains than genius"
and this judgment has won general approval. It should, however,
be considered in the light of what Silius was attempting. He would
recall the Roman taste to the classical integrity which he found in
the earlier epics. His opening lines are almost a declaration of his
purpose. Like Lucan, he follows the lead of Vergil, "I sing of
arms," but there the parallel ends. Lucan proceeds to pass moral
judgment on the events he is about to relate. Silius is objective. He
is also brief, as brief as Vergil. But, unlike Vergil, he announces
the second half of his subject, not as *the* hero but as the *heroes*.
There lay his great handicap: his epic had only historical, not
dramatic unity. It was perforce annalistic.

I sing of arms by which Aeneas' race
Won heaven-high glory when proud Carthage bowed
Before the laws of Rome. Grant, Muse, the power
To tell the tale of ancient Italy,
The heroes that she bore to wage her wars
When, false to its own word, the Cadmeian race
Sought to subdue her.

With real vigor Silius plunges into his story without any complimentary dedication or any flattery of the emperor and without
any philosophical or economic analysis of the subject in hand. This
contrast with Lucan is obvious and presumably intentional for
Silius deliberately takes sides against Lucan in the debatable and
debated question of the use of divine machinery in the epic. Lucan
had banished the gods in favor of extensive and melodramatic use
of omens, visions, dreams and sorcery. Silius does not renounce
these mainstays of rhetoric but he does revive the Olympians to
manipulate his action and interfere with its progress. Statius and

Valerius Flaccus were dealing with Greek myths and the gods were essentially part of the tradition. Silius was dealing with Roman history, not as with Vergil at the point where myth merges into historic tradition but at a stage when the facts were recorded in the Roman chronicles. His reactionary acceptance of the gods, not only controlling affairs but mingling with the human actors, was a brave but unhappy challenge to the poets of the rhetorical school. And with the gods come other traditional elements of the Vergilian epic: the funeral games, the visit to the shades of the lower world, the pictured shield, the catalogue of forces, some realistic, others unfortunately incongruous in a tale of historical warfare.

In spite of these handicaps, Silius maintained to a surprising degree his standard of direct narrative, untrammeled by the moralizing of the poet, the irrelevances of the rhetor and the polemics of the Stoic rebel. The first two books move with speed and considerable power. They take the story to the seige and fall of Saguntum. Then, through Spain and Gaul, over the Alps and into Italy, Hannibal's progress still holds the attention of the reader but the pace is slower and various digressions are introduced to compensate for the lack of interest in the tale itself. The story of Hercules depicted on the doors of the temple at Gades where Hannibal seeks knowledge of the future is somewhat irrelevant and completely so is the informative passage about the tides which follows closely after. But digressions are not disturbing until the campaign comes to a pause after the battle of Lake Trasimenus. Then in Book VI (101–551), carefully and logically introduced, comes the long story of Regulus. The period of Fabian delay is partly occupied by the story of the Fabii, a tale of Bacchus (Book VII) and the myth of the nymph Anna (Book VIII). These are all narrative digressions and none of them wholly irrelevant. Throughout the remaining nine books the history plods doggedly on and the author yields more and more to the temptation to relieve the monotony of his tale with the ornaments of rhetoric.

At this point it must be emphasized that Silius is, in many respects, more Ennian than Vergilian. True, all epic took a new start after Vergil's great accomplishment and no one can question the influence of the master on the work of Silius. But we have noted the essentially chronological, annalistic character of the *Punica*. In keeping with this, the narrative is for the most part plain, direct and swiftly moving. There is often an Homeric dignity and simplicity, quite foreign to the rhetorical epic, reminiscent of certain passages in Ennius. Two examples will suffice. The first is from Book XII.217ff, an account of the short career of Pedanius during the battle near Nola.

> His father was Eridanus, Venetian stock
> Produced him and the folk that boast
> The spring of Aponus. None equalled him
> They said, whether he called his troops to war
> Or peacefully worshipped the Muses when
> He chose the quiet of a poet's peace
> And with the Aonian harp softened life's toils.
> No youth was better known to Mars and none
> More loved of Phoebus. So as, with loosened rein
> He followed on the Carthaginian track
> And recognised the helm of Paulus slain—
> Young Cinyps, loved of Hannibal, was bearing it
> Proud of his master's weighty trust, no boy
> More fair to look upon, whose countenance
> Shone like the ivory constantly refreshed
> By Tibur's breeze or like the treasured pearl
> Torn from the Red Sea's waves and set in gold—
> And so when Pedianus saw the handsome lad
> Carrying the well known helmet with its crest
> As if the very ghost of Paulus' self
> Had suddenly appeared before his eyes
> From the infernal shades, claiming his arms,
> With shout of rage he charged. "Will you presume,
> You coward, to display the heraldry
> Of that most sacred head which even your chief
> Could never bear without the curse of heaven?
> Ho, Paulus!" From the shades, calling his ghost
> To witness, through the body of the boy
> The while he fled he plunged his fatal spear.

Then, leaping from his horse, with his right hand
He seized the mighty consul's helm and crest,
Despoiled the boy whose beauty fled in death.
The Stygian pallor robbed him of his flush,
The ambrosial locks lost lustre and the fair
Marmorial throat shrivelled in ugly death.
So when from Ocean's bed Lucifer comes
Showing to Venus all his new found flame
If there but come a sudden cloud, his light
Is dimmed, into the blackest shades of night
He sinks perforce his failing brilliancy.
Even so Pedianus as he seized the helm
And saw that countenance before him bared
Stood there astonished and restrained his wrath.

Forty lines later the episode closes in good heroic style.

An so to Nola's walls the Latin bands
Bearing their spoils with mighty shouts repair.

    The second illustration of what seems to me narrative more characteristic of Homer or Ennius than of their successors is the story of Murrus at Saguntum (I.376ff).

Before all others, in the bloom of youth,
Flashed Murrus, scion of Rutulian stock
(Yet from his mother Greek and blended so
Dulichian blood with Roman). Now he heard
The shouts of Aradus calling his friends
To help and where the corselet and the helm
Just failed to meet, wary, he thrust his spear
And o'er the prostrate form with mocking voice
"There now" he cried "thou liest, treacherous foe.
Thou wouldst be first to climb the Capitol
As victor. Whence so proud a prayer? Take now
Thy battle to the Stygian Jove." He spoke

And drove his spear deep in the Spaniard's thigh,
His heel upon the lips that sobbed in death.
One final taunt: "Here lies thy road to Rome,
So must thou hie thee on thy urgent way."

Admittedly, the matter of the tone and general character of these narratives is not strictly evidence: it involves the question of personal impression. This impression, furthermore, may result in part from an overestimation of the warmth of Silius' tribute to Ennius in Book XII.387ff.

I could not hope to tell these countless deaths
And deeds of horror worthily nor match
The passion of the warriors with my words.
But you, Calliope, endow my work
With power to tell the deeds too little known
Adown the ages that one hero wrought
And render worthy homage to a poet.
Ennius, scion of Messapus' royal line,
Fought at the front. Calabria's arid soil
Sent him to war, from ancient Rubiae.
(*Now* Rubiae is known for him alone.)
He, when the battle opened, had contrived
Conspicuous slaughter and his ardor grew
With each new death. Then Hostus, rushing in,
Seeking eternal fame could he but stay
The dreadful slaughter, mightily hurled his spear.
Apollo from a cloud laughed at his effort
And turned the weapon, useless, on the breeze.
Then spake: "This man is sacred, cherished by
The Aonian Sisters, poet whom Apollo loves.
He first shall sing in verse illustrious
The wars of Italy, extolling to the skies
Her leaders, shall make Helicon resound
With Latin measures, shall not yield in praise
To Ascra's bard." So Phoebus and a shaft
Pierced Hostus' temples twain with vengeance swift.

It may well be argued that Vergil also venerated Ennius and that he shows more direct borrowing from the earlier poet than does Silius. But the Ennian character of Silius' epic is more fundamental. In spite of his constant imitation of Vergil in details of composition, he reverted to the annalistic type of epic covering a long historical period in chronologically continuous narrative without the dramatic unity of the *Aeneid* with its single hero and its use of indirect narrative to cover antecedent events. A minor but impressive detail of Silius' reactionary tendency is his "old Roman" brand of Stoicism, reminiscent of the days of Ennius rather than those of Vergil or Lucan.

The Stoicism of Silius is well-attested and the reality of his faith was proven by his own suicide when life became intolerable. His is the Stoicism of Panaetius and the Scipionic Circle rather than that of the embattled reactionaries of Nero's day. Steep is the road of Virtue's progress (III.135); magnanimous Virtue knows not jealousy (XV.387); vain is superstition: the only goddess reigning in the warrior's heart is Virtue (V.126); for Virtue's self is its own finest reward (XIII.663); earth's first day determined its last (III.135); jealous Nature armed us with no greater boon than this, that the door of death lies open and gives us power to leave a life which is intolerable (XI.186). All of these are expressions of fundamental Stoicism rather than special barbs aimed at a hostile, non-Stoic authority. The same holds true of the attacks on luxury and unrestrained pleasure. They are general arraignments which might well have been written by a shocked conservative after the fall of Corinth and the sudden influx of wealth at Rome. Conspicuous is the long passage at the beginning of Book XV in which Voluptas and Virtus argue for the soul of young Scipio. Pleasure is given thirty-eight lines filled with alluring promises and her conclusion leaves no doubt that she is expressing the belief of the Epicurean.

> Hearken to me. Man's mortal span moves on
> And none is born again. The hours speed by,
> The stream of Tartarus bears him away
> Nor suffers him to take what here on earth

Has pleased his heart. What man can fail at death
To mourn too late rejection of my hours?

Virtue, however, in fifty-two lines, refutes the arguments of Pleasure and convinces young Scipio.

Then, when thy country's need shall summon thee,
Thou shalt be first in arms, the first to scale
The hostile wall, turned not by sword or gold.
Hence shalt thou win, not garments dipped in dyes
Of Tyre, nor gifts of fragrant myrrh beneath
Man's dignity. Nay, I will give to thee
Victory over him who now assails
Thy sovereign power and thou shalt dedicate
To Jove proud plunder of the slaughtered foe.

Pleasure has, nevertheless, the last word and makes a prophecy which does smack of contemporary satire.

That day shall come when Rome to my commands
Shall yield obedience, rejoice to serve,
And honor shall be paid to me alone.

One more illustration will suffice to indicate the quality of Silius' belief. It is closer to the New Testament than to the Satiric rejection of wealth. Volunx, one of the victims of the battle of Lake Trasumennus, is addressed by the poet (V.261ff):

You too are slain nor all your hoarded wealth
Availed you aught, nor royal palace decked
With ivory. What profit now the gold
Of plundered peoples? Him whom yesterday
Fortune o'erwhelmed with riches piled high
And gifts supreme, to-day shall Charon's self
Ferry all naked in his Stygian skiff.

This personal intrusion of the poet to address a character in the epic is not altogether typical of Silius. Vergil had not as completely as Homer refrained from the personal comment but his first person intrusions were rare. So were those of Silius. Scarcely more than half a dozen times does he comment in person and he does not devise methods of disguising personal comment. This is in sharp contrast with Lucan who was constantly the showman, persistently explaining, although he actually speaks in the first person only in his first hundred lines.

The general character of Silius' epic is clear. It is annalistic in form, "old Roman" in spirit and, at least to a limited extent, reactionary in relation to the rhetoric and satire of the first century. It is not unfair to say that it is uninspired. The brief and forceful introduction gave promise of something better than was possible of attainment, at least by Silius. The difficulty of his problem appears vividly at the conclusion of the poem. The subject had been announced as arms and the heroes who conquered Carthage. But an epic craves a hero. Hannibal had been introduced in the opening lines, taking his grim oath of vengeance against Rome. This was part of the motivation of the epic, but it gave a powerful impetus to the reader's interest in young Hannibal. Furthermore, he was destined to be the only human character surviving the seventeen books. And so, at line 604 of the final book we find the real conclusion of the epic, not in the death but in the withdrawal of Hannibal.

> Then Juno, grieving, sought her celestial home
> And as the foe approached to mount the hill
> Hannibal spake to his own heart: "If all
> The universe shall crash and heaven fall
> Upon this head, if earth shall yawn, even so
> Thou canst not, Jupiter, wipe Cannae out
> For ages still to come. Sooner thou'lt lose
> Thy mighty power than ever men forget
> The name and deeds of Hannibal. Thou, Rome,
> Shalt not be safe from me when I am gone.
> I shall survive my country and shall live

A threat of war for thee. Now for a while
Thou art the victor and thine enemies
Yield to Rome's arms. Enough revenge for me
That Dardan mothers and the Italian folk
Shall live in dread so long as I shall live,
Shall know no peace of heart—expecting me."
So, with a pitiful remnant, Hannibal
Withdrew to hiding. And the war was done.

This, if it were the actual end of the poem, would recall the death of Turnus and the final line of the *Aeneid*. But the dramatic conclusion of Vergil's poem had been prepared for and Aeneas was in fact the hero and the future of Rome was assured. Hannibal had usurped the position of hero and had evaded death. Desperately Silius attempts to retrieve his position and to put Scipio into the place of honor.

So the war ended. To the Ausonian chief
Gates of the citadel are opened wide,
The vicious rites and arms removed and laws
Inscribed. The power of arrogant wealth was crushed,
The mighty towers laid low. Then the tall ships,
Put to the torch, produced a spectacle
For Carthage. With a sudden breeze the sea
Itself burst into flame: Nereus turned pale
Before that blaze of devastating light.
But he, the peerless general, first to win
A surname from the land he overthrew,
Clothed in a glory that should live for ay,
Serene in power, o'er the blue sea returned
To Rome, proudly to ride as conqueror
In lofty triumph to his ancestral home.

Then follows, unhappily, the list of prisoners who graced the triumph—but only the statue of Hannibal—and finally the conqueror.

He rides
On high, bedecked with purple and with gold,
His Martian features welcome to the crowd
Of citizens, as Liber in his car
By tigers drawn from India's spicy shores
Or as Tyrinthius o'er the Phlegraean plain,
The giants conquered, touched the stars of heaven.
Hail, sire invisible that shall not yield
Even to Quirinus, nevermore give place
To brave Camillus, not in worth or fame.
Never shall Rome prove false in naming thee
Offspring of her Tarpeian Thunderer.

It is an unsatisfactory conclusion to an instructive failure.
Silius was obviously not enough of a poet to accomplish what he
desired but his very lack of success throws light on the epics which
had greater success in his era. Nor did he succeed in avoiding
much at which he seemed to rebel. He avoided elaborate and extended descriptions but occasionally rivalled the rhetoricians with
a descriptive tone-setting passage such as that describing the scene
of Hannibal's famous oath taking. (I.80ff.)

Within the city's midst there stands a shrine
To Dido's spirit consecrate, imbued with all
The awe of Tyrian gloom. Box trees and pine
With darkling shadows circle it and hide
The light of heaven. Here in ages past
The Queen had freed herself from mortal woes.
Dark marbles, effigies of ancient kings,
Stand in long lines: proud Belus and his sons,
Agenor, glory of the race, and next
Phoenix that left an ageless name, the Queen
Dido herself, linked for eternity
With great Sychaeus, at her feet there lies
A sword of Phrygian make. And then appear
A hundred altars to the gods above
And to the Lords of Hell, in serried ranks.

With locks dishevelled, in her Stygian garb,
The priestess calls the powers of Acheron.
Earth groans as through the darkling shadows bursts
The horrid Sibyl. With unkindled fires
The altars flame.

With greater success Silius avoided the *sententia* and sharply pointed phrase and apostrophes are not common. A prophetic soldier in V.63 reminds us of Lucan's raving women at the gate of Rome and Silius does not hesitate to make generous use of omens in addition to his divine machinery. Learning intrudes but rarely: the tides in Book III, elephants in Book IX and worldwide customs of burial in Book XIII are conspicuous. Otherwise digressions consist of narrative, are interesting on their own account and are reasonably relevant. The melodramatic description of horrors is more frequent in spite of some apparent attempt at restraint. The worst instance (VI.41ff) may stand for all.

                      Hard by appeared
Such dedicated madness as demands
The eulogy of song. Laevinus there,
Scion of old Privernus, lay half dead
Upon his dying victim, Nasamon.
No spear had he, no sword; in the affray
Fortune had taken all. Yet, stripped of all,
His rage equipped him: with his bloody jaws
He fought—his teeth served anger as a sword.
Now the torn nostrils, now the mangled eyes
He gnawed.

The details continue but may best be left to the imagination. It must have required considerable effort for the polished old gentleman, living so much as he did in the past of Vergil and Cicero, not to overlook Ennius and Scipio, to make such concession to contemporary taste.

CHAPTER TEN

Juvenal

THE AGE OF RHETORIC in Roman poetry came to its real end with
two great writers of curiously contrasted characteristics: Juvenal
the satirist with too much anger in his make-up to be dominated
by rhetoric; and Martial the epigrammatist with too much sense of
humor. They also mark the close of a literary era, that era which
began when the satirist Lucilius, the epigrammatist Catullus, and
the epic poet Lucretius ventured to introduce the personal element
into Roman poetry and to free it from the bonds of traditionalism.
Two centuries had seen tremendous change and growth in the
product but these two later writers have no hesitation in an-
nouncing the original source of their compositions. In his introductory satire Juvenal first gives a suitable satiric reason for
writing at all: reprisal against the poets who constantly deafen him
with the old rhetorical stuff. He winds up his opening paragraph:

> The reason why
> I chose the course where once the foster son
> Of proud Aurunca drove his noble steeds
> If you have leisure and will hear, I'll tell.

After twenty-nine lines, summarizing in vivid, scathing words some
of the evils of his day which rouse his ire, he says:

> Are these foul doings uncongenial stuff
> For the Venusian spotlight? Shall I not
> Attack them rather than pursue the tale
> Of Hercules or Diomede or the groans

Issuing from the Cretan labyrinth?
Should I be busy with the futile myth
Of flying Daedalus and his fallen son
While pander husbands reap the price of shame?

And so he launches into twenty-three more lines of bitter invective which concludes with the famous line, "If nature will not, indignation will / produce the verse I write."

Little is known with surety of the life of Juvenal. There are many lives in the manuscripts but they are late and give strong indication of having been drawn with some imagination from the satires themselves. Aquinum would seem to have been his birthplace and the date of his birth somewhere in the neighborhood of 60 A.D. He must have been reasonably well-to-do for he mentions three homes, one each at Rome, Aquinum and Tibur and his hatred of foreigners and freedmen suggests that he was a free Roman citizen of Italian blood with something of Tacitus' nostalgic reverence for the "olden days." His satires were published in successive books from 100 to 128 A.D. There is no doubt whatever that he had the normal training in rhetoric and, in his early days, declaimed with enthusiasm. He was disgusted with the unreality and preciosity of the current rhetorical poetry but never failed to make use of his training in the more striking methods of the schools.

Juvenal's published work as it has come down to us consists of fifteen satires and an unfinished sixteenth, comprising five books. As we have seen, he claimed Lucilius and Horace as his models; for his subject matter he conceived an even wider range than theirs.

Since when Deucalion saw the rising flood,
Scaled the high mountain in his little ark
And sought new prophecies, when one by one
The stones drew breath and life and Pyrrha showed
The new-made naked females to their mates,
All that men do, their hopes, their fears, their wrath,
Their pleasures too, their gaddings all about,
Shall be the hodge-podge of my little book.

But his point of view is not actually so all-embracing. This he
makes clear in what immediately follows. It is not *all* of life which
he would make his subject but the more vicious phases of life.

> And when, I ask you, has a greater crop
> Of vices sprung to life? What other day
> Has seen a greater splurge of avarice?

To Juvenal satire is the scourge of vice. He has none of Horace's
genial view of the world about him nor any of Persius' moral
earnestness in propagating the Stoic faith. Such philosophy as he
expresses is certainly Stoic but he resembles far more the Cynic
preacher of hell fire on the street corner than the arm chair philosopher. He is really neither. He is the angry protesting victim of
a society which to him appears to be almost wholly vile, but his
protest seems often to be not so much against the moral implica-
tions of vice as against the discomfort and degradation which it
inflicts on men like himself. Like Lucan with his personal political
fanaticism, Juvenal, with his personal hatred of a degenerate
society, brings to the aid of his denunciation all the weapons of
rhetoric wielded with the skill of a sincere and infuriated expert.

There is a further special interest in Juvenal's own introduction
to his satires for he expresses there in no uncertain terms his dissatisfaction with the detachment of contemporary poetry from the
immediate realities of life, a dissatisfaction akin to that of the
young neoterics of Catullus' day. It is therefore worth quoting at
some length.

> Forever must I listen? Nevermore
> Avenge the pain of Cordus' rhetoric?
> Without reprisal shall each upstart poet
> Bedin my ears with elegy and play?
> Without reprisal shall my days be stolen
> By Telephus in rags, Orestes mad,
> Besmearing margin, title page and blanks
> And still unfinished? No man knows so well
> His hearth and home as I the grove of Mars

Or Vulcan's cavern by the Aeolian rocks,
The business of the winds, what hapless shades
Aeacus tortures in the shadowy realms,
Or whence those ancient uncouth mariners
Reclaimed the blessed fleece, what ashen shafts
Monychus wields—all these the marble halls
Of Fronto and his plane tree shout to heaven,
And columns ruptured by the reader's rage.
One music issues from poets great and small.
I too have felt the rhetor's rod; I too
Have given advice to Sulla to withdraw
To private slumber. Stupid clemency
Alone could bid me face the mob of poets
And spare the parchment. But the reason why
I choose the course where once the foster son
Of proud Aurunca drove his noble steeds
If you have leisure and will hear, I'll tell.

Juvenal gives also a preview of the factors in contemporary life
which are to be the targets of his attack. In the best satiric manner he does this by means of concrete examples rather than by
generalizations.

When eunuchs turn to wedlock, when the boar
Is hunted by a Mevia with breast bared
To wield the spear, when one who was a barber,
The while my beard was growing, now outstrips
In wealth Rome's greatest bluebloods . . .

and so on through a picture gallery of foppish foreigners, the
newly rich, informers battening on their so-called friends, gigolos
despoiling old women, venal politicians, effeminate members of
the younger generation, forgers of wills, husband poisoners. Then,
with characteristic satiric epigram, he sums it all up: Integrity is
praised—and left to shiver in neglect. In one way or another money
is at the root of all these evils but each mercenary evil is made

vivid by the bold strokes which paint its particular devotees. The examples may be fictitious or drawn from the preceding generation, but they are all contemporary in their implication.

In the second satire Juvenal follows the lead of Horace who published, next to his introduction, his one (to us) thoroughly indecent satire, brilliant but embarrassing in its pornographic frankness. It was presumably a bid for attention. So Juvenal selects for second place a subject which was bound to attract a considerable audience, the prevalence of sexual vice, especially unnatural vice. Whatever the judgment on his taste, his skill as an artist must have won the critics' praise.

The third satire shows an increased care for the dramatic setting and construction, greater than that of any other satire. The author's old friend Umbricius, unable to endure longer the discomforts of the city, is preparing to move to Cumae and, while his household belongings are being loaded onto a wagon at the Porta Capena, he holds forth to Juvenal on the reasons for his departure. In the closing lines of the satire the loading is completed and farewells are said. The preamble is developed with care and furnishes one of the rare expressions in the work of Juvenal of any appreciation of nature. (I.3.1–20.)

> Distressed as I must be to lose a friend
> Long tried, I can but envy one who goes
> To fix his home at idle Cumae, thus
> Adding one neighbor to the Sibyl's shore.
> There is the gate to Baiae, a retreat
> All loveliness. And even Prochyta
> Is better than Subura, for what waste
> Of solitude, what wretched spot of earth
> Would you not welcome rather than endure
> Daily the fear of fire or the collapse
> Of buildings and the dangers numberless
> That haunt the city—or the droning poets
> Reciting in the dog-days? But the while
> His household goods entire were being heaped

On one small wagon, by the dripping arch
That spans the Capena gate, Umbricius stood
And waited. There where ancient Numa once
Kept assignation with Egeria,
The sacred spring, the grove, the hallowed shrine
Are rented out to Jews who come in flocks
With picnic baskets. Every tree must yield
Its profit while the ejected Muses beg.
Down to the spring we strolled through curious caves
That Nature never wrought. How much more real
The presence of the nymph if Nature's green
Margined the waters and the native rock
Were undefiled by marble colonnades.

The setting of the satire is completed in the last eight lines with a nice variation. This closing half of the framework is brief, as so often in Horace, and is not spoken directly by Juvenal but is incorporated into the discourse of Umbricius which forms the body of the satire.

I am not done: the tale is endless, but
The mules are restless and the sun is low.
I must be off. The driver cracks his whip.
Farewell. Remember your old friend and when
Rome sends you to Aquinum for a rest
Invite me over to your hallowed shore
From my plain Cumae. If these irk you not
I'll add more satires to this homely crop.

Within the picturesque framework, Umbricius develops two fundamental complaints which he has against Rome, the intrusion of Greeks and other foreigners into every phase of Roman life and the physical discomforts and dangers of the city. Behind both complaints is the basic grievance that money, however gained, has become all powerful while honest worth counts for nothing. (III.21ff.)

At last Umbricius spoke: Since in the town
There is no longer place for honesty
And no reward for toil, what yesterday
Possessed is less to-day and will be less
To-morrow, I am off to where long since
Daedalus laid aside his weary wings.
While still not every hair is grey and while
Old age has yet to bend me and some thread
Remains for Lachesis to spin, before
My feet refuse to carry me without
Support, I'll leave my country. Catulus,
Artorius, let them live there and all
That can turn black to white nor hesitate
To take the city contracts to repair
Rome's public buildings or collect the toll
By river bridge or harbor, or to dredge
The sewers, conduct Rome's funerals and at last
Go bankrupt at a profit. These fine sirs
Were once the mountebanks blowing their horns
At country fairs, who now give lavish games
And when the crowd so wills with downturned thumb
Kill off the gladiators with a smile.
Then home to clean the municipal latrines.

The first specification of Umbricius' arraignment of contemporary Rome deals with the eastern immigrant. His complaint is that the honest native-born son of Rome cannot compete in the struggle for subsistence with the clever and wholly unscrupulous immigrant. But incidentally there is insistent reference to their favorite means of support, the reward of shameless toadying to the rich. (III.58ff.)

Who 'tis makes captives of our mighty rich,
Whom chiefly I'd escape, I will confess
Nor blush to tell. Oh, Romans, countrymen,
I cannot stand a Grecian Rome. And yet
What portion of our dregs is truly Greek?

Syrian Orontes has for many a day
Been emptying its bilge into our Tiber,
Bringing its speech and all its customs vile,
Its harps and pipes, its native tambourines,
The girls for auctioning on circus days:
"Who'll buy a barbarian whore with turban gay?"
Quirinus, that stout farmer lad of your's
To-day wears a Greek dinner coat; around
His neck, perfumed of course, Greek garlands hang.
Yon fellow comes from lofty Sicyon,
That one from Alabandi, Amydon
Gave birth to this, another Samos bore,
Tralles or Andros, but each mother's son
Makes for the Esquiline or Viminal
There to become the trusted confidante
Of our great blue-bloods—and their master too.
Nimble the Grecian wit, his boldness past
Control, his speech fluent as Isaeus' was.
What do you think him? Everything in one
He brings us: scholar, critic, robber, priest,
Circus performer, doctor, soothsayer too:
Yon hungry little Greek knows everything.

The latter half of the third satire is more appealing to the modern reader, dealing as it does with the concrete discomforts of a crowded metropolis. Perhaps the most vivid picture is that of a tenement fire in Rome with its stress on the callous attitude toward the poor. (III.190ff.)

Who e'er at cool Praeneste or along
The wooded ridge of high Volsinii
Or in such simple towns as Gabii
And Tibur fears collapsing tenements?
Rome for the most part balances herself
Precariously on slender props installed
By agents whose ingenious artifice
Conceals the gaping cracks and bids us rest

Secure while dire catastrophe impends.
My mind's made up to live where neither fire
Threatens my peace nor terrors of the night.
Ucalegon shouts "Water!" and removes
His few belongings; three floors burn below
And you lie ignorant. While panic reigns
The last to burn is he whose humble home
Only the tiles keep dry, up where the doves
Bestow their eggs. Codrus possessed a bed
Too small for Procula, six jugs to adorn
His simple sideboard and a drinking cup,
One ornament, a Chiron in repose,
One ancient chest of learned literature
Gnawed by barbarian mice. Who would deny
Codrus had nothing? Yet poor Codrus lost
All of that nothing. And the final blow
Falls when thus stripped he begs a crust and finds
None that will help him with a bite to eat
Or home to cover him. Yet, if the house
Of great Asturicus has gone, the town
Wears mourning and the judge adjourns the court.
Then 'tis we groan at Rome's unhappy state,
Lament the evil chance. The fire still burns
While citizens come running with relief.
Money pours in, one sympathizer brings
A fair white statue in the nude, another
The ancient trappings of the Asian gods.
Books and a bookcase speedily appear
Complete with a Minerva and a peck
Of solid silver. Persicus, the flower
Supreme of childless nabobs, furnishes
His house with rich donations far beyond
His losses till the whispering gossips say
He must have touched the conflagration off.

Even more dramatic is the vignette of a traffic accident, sixty-four lines later.

One passing dray carries a mighty fir
Swaying on high, the next a towering pine,
Threatening our heads. And if the mountainous load
Of marble from another should upset
Upon the road, what of our bodies then?
Who would collect our bones? Gone like the breath
Of life is every victim from the herd
Of common folk. Meanwhile, all unconcerned,
His household scours the platters, pokes the fires,
Lays out the greasy strigils, flask of oil
And ample bath towel. While they bustle on
The master sits beside the Styx and views
The horrid ferryman with never a hope
Of passage o'er the muddy stream, poor man,
For none has put a penny in his mouth.

This is followed by another quick but vivid shot at the danger
from an accidental crash or the casual disposal of refuse from the
high windows of a tenement. (III.268ff.)

Glance now at dangers of another sort:
The lofty buildings whence a broken pot
May crush your cranium as it hurtles down
To dent the pavement. You would be a fool
Improvident to make your thoughtless way
To dinner without first making your will.
You face as many threats of sudden death
As there are windows and your only prayer
That they may be content merely to dump
The contents of their slop jars on your head.

If the passing citizen escapes all of these threats he is likely to
fall victim to a band of prowling thugs. This whole presentation is
made with satiric exaggeration, but Dr. Johnson found it realistic
enough to adapt it closely in his "London" and neither Roman nor
Londoner would seem to have found the picture beyond recognition.

The fourth satire is a burlesque account of an emergency meeting of Domitian's cabinet to decide on the disposition of an oversize fish caught in the Adriatic and presented by the fisherman to the emperor to escape charges on the part of some informer that the fish came from the royal preserves. The vivid pen pictures of the fawning counsellors give the satirist ample opportunity for incidental arraignment of specific vices, but the special brilliance of the satire lies in the summary descriptions of the individual members of the board. Pegasus, the newly made *vilicus* of the city (a *vilicus* was the overseer of the slaves on a farm), "the sweet old age of Crispus whose character was as soft as his eloquence," Crispinus "sweating with morning perfume to outsmell two funeral processions," Pompeius who cut throats in a whisper, Veiento, the blind flatterer who looks to the left as he lauds the fish on his right, Rubrius more shameless than a pimp writing satire, the stomach of Montanus, slow of abdomen. The solemn decision is that a platter large enough for the fish be made forthwith and that in the future official potters always attend the emperor. The skit is introduced by an overlong attack on Crispinus, a servile immigrant from Egypt grown rich and powerful in Rome. He ostentatiously paid a fabulous price for a fish; if a mere courtier does that what shall we think of the emperor's gluttony?

> Begin, Calliope, but seat yourself.
> No song is here, a plain unvarnished tale.
> Sing on, Pierides, and may it help
> My case that you girls are the speakers here.

Juvenal's light touch is that of a mastodon but it indicates that he is attempting something different from his ordinary fulmination. The conclusion of the satire (144ff) is in the more familiar tone.

> The council rises, ordered to depart,
> Those leaders of the state whom the great chief
> Had called astonished and in furious haste
> As though to hear some news about the war
> In Germany or learn the vital facts

Brought from the ends of earth in some despatch
On anxious wing. Would god that he had given
To trifles such as this those cruel hours
That robbed the city of great souls and true
With no constraint and no avenging hand.
But he did meet his fate when terror reached
The working man—that was his end whose hands
Dripped with the blood of Rome's aristocrats.

The attacks on vice are resumed in the fifth satire, the target
here being the rich man who invites to his table his lesser friends
and dependents and serves them an inferior menu while he himself consumes the best on the market. Juvenal is scathing in his
treatment of Virro, the host, but the satire is ostensibly aimed at
the shameless guest, for there is here once more a framework
within which the satire is set and it attacks with scorn the victim
of Virro's snobbery. (V.1ff and V.170ff.)

If you are unashamed and still believe
That bids to dinner are the highest good,
Can bear such insults as Sarmentus spurned
At Caesar's table and vile Gabba scorned,
I'll never take your evidence on oath.

* * * * *

He knows what he is doing for 'tis not
Unwittingly he treats you as he does.
If you can bear it you deserve it all.
You'll bow your shaven head to well earned blows
Nor cringe at outrage, worthy as you are
Of such a dinner and of such a friend.

Satire VI does for the female what Satire II had done for the
male. It is a gallery of bad women. Here Juvenal found a wholly
congenial subject and developed it into his longest satire. He addresses it to a friend, Postumus, who to Juvenal's horror seems to
be contemplating marriage. The introduction is characteristic: Ju-

venal gives his version of the three ages of the world but it is confined to their decline in sexual morality.

> Shame lingered, so I take it, on the earth
> Long years in Saturn's ancient reign the while
> Chill caves provided humble homes and gave
> Common asylum to the hearth and fire,
> The household god, the master and the flocks.
> The rustic wife spread there a brushwood bed
> Covered with hides of neighboring wild beasts,
> A wife unlike you, Cynthia, or you
> Whose glittering eyes a sparrow's death bedimmed,
> Oft rougher than her acorn-belching swain.
> For men lived otherwise when earth was new
> And heaven was young, men sprung from cloven oak
> Or molded clay, who knew no ancestors.
> Traces there were of ancient shame when next
> Jove ruled the world (but Jove without a beard)
> Ere Greeks had learned to swear by others' heads,
> When none feared thieves among the garden truck,
> Living with field and orchard all unfenced.
> But then Astraea step by step withdrew
> To heaven, an outlaw with her sister Shame.
> 'Tis ancient practice, Postumus, to foul
> Another's marriage couch and scorn the god
> Of sacred union. Other crimes the age
> Of iron would produce; the silver years
> First saw adultery. Yet in our day
> You plan a wedding contract and the rites
> Of wedlock, hie you to a barber, give
> A ring as pledge. Surely you once were sane:
> Will you then, Postumus, marry a wife?
> Tell me, what writhing snakes of madness, what
> Tisiphone bedevils you, can you
> Brook any mistress while there's rope at hand
> And windows high aloft from which to plunge?
> And while the Aemilian Bridge awaits hard by?

The catalogue of bad women is all-embracing for Juvenal's wrath is not confined to the immoral: it includes the gossip, the masterful woman, the athletic girl, the educated wife who prates Vergil and compares his art with Homer's, the mother-in-law and even what we may call the good woman in the worst sense of the word. (VI.161ff.)

> "Of womankind does none seem worthy then?"
> Be she all fair and comely, fruitful, rich,
> With ancestors galore, more chaste than those
> Famed Sabine matrons with dissheveled locks
> Who split the battle lines, a bird as rare
> On earth as is the fabulous black swan:
> Who can endure a wife endowed with all
> The virtues? Venustina I prefer
> To you, Cornelia, mother of those two
> Notorious Gracchi, if with all your pride
> You bring as dowry haughty arrogance
> And family triumphs. Take away, I pray,
> Your Hannibal and Syphax' conquered camp:
> Begone with all your Carthage.

So full of his subject is Juvenal that he follows no systematic plan but pours forth his fury in an unfailing stream of vivid characterization. One qualifying distinction he does make in his abrupt conclusion: he can look with less violent resentment on the outrages which are inspired by furious passion than on those which result from deliberate and apparently sane decision. (VI.651ff.)

> 'Tis her who weighs the price I cannot brook,
> With calculating mind commits the crime.
> Upon the stage they watch Alcestis die
> To save her husband: give them that same choice,
> They'd sacrifice their husbands for a pup.
> You'll always meet some Danaid murderess,
> Some Eriphyle: every little town
> Has its own Clytemnestra; but the first

Tyndaris wielded by hand a foolish axe:
'Tis smoother now, done with a snake's entrails.
But she'll use axe if her Atreides finds
The Pontic cure of that thrice conquered king.

The seventh and eighth satires relieved the poet's mind of two other burdens, his resentment at the lack of appreciation shown toward literary aspirants and the degeneracy of the nobility. Critics have spoken highly of the noble sentiments of Satire VIII but the tone is the normal tone of satire and the virtuous ideals, while sound, are scarcely profound. The philosophy is of the Poor Richard variety and the real enthusiasm of the writer is expended on the vices exhibited by members of the old Roman families, particular examples taken from the reign of Nero. Satire IX is also undistinguished. It depicts the remorse of one who looks back upon a misspent life. It is usually grouped with the second and sixth because of its sexual outspokenness, but it lacks the vigor and distinction of those tirades against man and woman. These three satires form Book III and the date of their publication is uncertain. It would appear that Juvenal was losing with age some of the fine indignation which inspired his earlier invectives and this is to a degree borne out by a study of the later satires.

Not that his ability was failing. Satire X is perhaps his best, certainly the most successful, for it is still the best known. Partly this is due to Dr. Johnson's imitation, "The Vanity of Human Wishes." But conversely, be it noted, the popularity of Dr. Johnson's masterpiece is largely due to the brilliance of Juvenal's original. The satire is long, 366 lines, but carefully constructed with eloquent preface and conclusion and an orderly sequence of ideas. The mature Juvenal is scarcely less pessimistic than his earlier self but he is less flamboyantly indignant at the world and he introduces at least a few lines of constructive thought in his closing paragraph. He has by no means lost the power of vividly portraying the ills of life but there is less wild exaggeration: his examples, if no less horrifying are more realistic for the average man. In general there is more restraint in the piling up of illustrations although there is still too much of this for modern taste. Such epigrams as "No poison draught is drunk from pottery" season the satire and some of the word pictures are unforgettable. The introduction suggests the plan of the satire. (X.1ff and 23ff.)

> In every land from Gades in the west
> To where the dawn breaks over Ganges, few
> There be who can, free from the clouds of error,
> Distinguish true good from its opposite.
> What, with sound reason, do we fear or hope?
> What do you ever undertake with such
> Auspicious start that you do not repent
> The issue of your act? Whole families
> Complacent gods have wrecked through their own prayers.
> Toga and uniform, pregnant with fate,
> Men crave. The power of speech, high eloquence
> Have proven fatal and the very strength
> In which one puts his faith has wrought his death.
> Far more are strangled by the wealth compiled
> With anxious care and bank accounts as much
> Beyond all possible inheritance
> As British whales outstrip our dolphins' size.

*   *   *   *   *

> The best know prayers
> At every shrine are prayers for wealth, that our
> Account may grow till it becomes the first
> In all the forum. Yet, no poison draught
> Is drunk from pottery: fear *that* what time
> You raise a jewelled cup or Setine wine
> Glows in a golden goblet.

In almost Horatian manner Juvenal introduces the laughing Democritus and the weeping Heracleitus, commending their attitude toward mankind, and continues:

> What *are* the prayers then, vain or dangerous?
> And for what blessings *should* we beg the gods?

The foolish prayer which he develops first is the prayer for political power and his example of its fatal danger is the fall of
Sejanus which may well serve to illustrate his use of the concrete.

> Power political breeds jealousy,
> Hurling its victim down: the glorious page
> Of honors ends in ruin. Statues fall,
> Ropes drag them off, the axes pulverise
> The chariot wheels, the horses' innocent legs;
> That head the people worshipped glows red hot:
> Mighty Sejanus crackles. So there come,
> From that face second in the whole wide world,
> Jugs, slop-jars, frying pans and chamber pots.
> Hang laurels on your door, lead the white bull
> Up to the Capitol: Sejanus' self
> Is·dragged off by the hook for all to see.
> Rejoicing everywhere. "Look at those lips;
> Oh, what a face was that. Upon my word,
> I never loved the man. But what the charge?
> Who the informer? Who the witnesses?"
> "Nothing like that. A weighty letter came
> From Capri." "Fair enough: I ask no more.
> But what of Remus' folk?" "They follow fate
> As always, hate the man who's down. This folk,
> If Nortia had preferred the Tuscan Knight
> And the old Emperor, caught off his guard,
> Had been the one to fall, at this same hour
> Would hail Sejanus with Augustus' name."

After political power comes eloquence with Cicero and Demosthenes as examples of its unhappy results. Then military success,
featuring Hannibal and Alexander. The account of Hannibal's
march on Rome winds up with a characteristic Juvenalian
apostrophe.

> Madman, go
> Charging the cruel Alps to make yourself
> A tale for puling schoolboys to recite.

Next come the prayers for long life. Priam and Nestor, Marius and Pompey serve to illustrate the unhappiness of too long life, but they are far less impressive than the description of old age itself in which Juvenal is at his fiendish best.

> In youth, we know
> Variety's the law: one's handsomer
> Than is another, one man's strong, another frail;
> Old age is all one ilk. The voice that shakes
> As shake the legs, as shakes the wobbling head;
> The second infancy of dripping nose,
> The munch of bread by gums untennanted,
> Till he becomes a burden to his wife,
> His children and himself that would disgust
> Even a flatterer of Cossus' stamp.
> His torpid palate relishes no more
> The joys of wine and food. Forgotten now
> The flame of love—if not forgotten, lost.
> Look at another sense destroyed: what joy
> For him in music of the lyre even if
> Seleucus sing or other glittering star?
> What matter where he's seated at the show
> Who scarce can hear the horns or tuba's blast?
> His boy must shout to make him hear the names
> Of callers or to tell the time of day.
> Scarce any drop of blood in his chill frame
> That only fever warms, while round him dance
> A chorus of diseases. Ask their names:
> I'd sooner list the fools that Oppia loved,
> How many patients Themison has killed
> This autumn.

This is not all but it is probably enough. After the prayers for long life come those of parents that their children may be beautiful. The illustrations of fatal beauty are Lucretia and Verginia, Hippolytus and Bellerophon. And so on to his conclusion.

Shall man then pray for nothing? If you want
Advice from me you'll leave it to the gods
Themselves to give what is expedient
For us and our affairs. The gods will grant
Not what is pleasant but most suitable.
Dearer to them is man than to himself.
We are led on by blind impulse or greed
To pray for wife or offspring; *they* know well
What kind of wife 'twould be, what kind of sons.
But, if you needs must make some prayer and bring
The entrails to the altar with your gift
Of blessed white pig sausage, then, I say,
Pray for a sound mind in a body sound.
Ask for a bouyant heart that fears not death,
That counts our span of life among the gifts
Of Nature, that can bear what toils may come,
That knows not anger nor too much desire,
That would prefer the toils of Hercules
To love and banqueting in Ninevah.

The remaining satires come as an anti-climax after the tenth. Eleven is an invitation to a simple dinner in the country but without the conviction which Horace put into similar invitations and dwelling too long on the contrasting luxuries of city feasts. Twelve is a thanksgiving poem on the occasion of his friend arriving safely home from a sea voyage, marred by the poet's protest that he is not trying to win favor and reward from Catullus. Thirteen is a *consolatio* addressed to Calvinus who has been cheated out of ten thousand sesterces. It is hard to avoid a suspicion of irony in the comfort given—such loss is an everyday occurrence and a guilty conscience will sufficiently avenge the act. Fourteen is an appeal to fathers to set good examples for their sons who will be bad enough by nature. Avarice is the vice chiefly attacked. Fifteen is partly narrative, the account of an Egyptian case of cannabalism, and sixteen, incomplete, is an arraignment of the unfair advantages enjoyed by soldiers.

Juvenal never exploited his own life and characteristics in his writings and these can therefore be studied and evaluated without prejudice arising from a knowledge of the facts of his life. For there is no dependable evidence from other sources to justify any biographical assumptions. To assume a given type of disposition for a writer of satire because of the tone of his published work is absurd. The sixteen satires do, however, take a definite position in literary history.

The independence of the author in expressing his personal opinion is taken for granted with a certain limitation forcibly applied by the tyranny of one-man power. This despotic supervision is reflected in all the attacks on the government which the transition from Domitian to the Ulpian emperors make it possible to deliver. The pessimism of the opposition to imperial power produced the atmosphere of desperation so unlike the calm of Horace's criticisms which seem optimistic by contrast. The same condition would account for the contrast between Horace's genial wit and the caustic irony of Juvenal. Between the two the academic seriousness of Persius pales into obscurity.

From another angle, Horace's satires exhibit a naturalness which came from the forward looking enthusiasm of the Augustan milieu; Persius represents the rhetoric of the schools at the peak of its influence with the quality of the product determined by its reception at the hands of a recitation audience. In Juvenal, the influence of the rhetoricians has been to a large degree assimilated. Its devices have become part of the equipment of the writer but the writer has shaken off the dominance of the school teacher. Juvenal is master of the epigrammatic phrase, the *sententia* of the rhetorician. He makes frequent use of apostrophe and rhetorical questions. To some degree the parts are still developed and polished to the detriment of the whole. Mythological and historical allusion is often too frequent and too obscure. But there is regard for the unity of individual satires, an individuality in their composition and a lack of formal restraint which seems to indicate the end of rhetorical artificiality. Juvenal marked the last stage of development in the Roman Satire in verse motivated by a powerful indignation and expressed in language adequate to the motivation.

CHAPTER ELEVEN

Martial

MARTIAL, THE EPIGRAMMATIST Marcus Valerius Martialis, came from the mining town of Bilbilis in Spain. His claim to Iberian details in his appearance is probably to be attributed to his satiric humor: his name implies respectable Roman ancestry and his parents saw to it that he had a good Roman education to which he refers with the same satiric whimsicality:

> My silly parents taught me cultured ways
> But what have I to do with pedagogues
> Or rhetoricians?

In his early twenties he moved to Rome where one emigré from the Spanish province, Seneca, was a minister of Nero and another, Lucan, was the leading poet of the day. They can hardly have been the help to Martial which he may have expected, for both fell in the Pisonian conspiracy shortly after his arrival in Rome.

Martial was not, however, one to be readily crushed. There is no evidence that he ever suffered from poverty and the charges against him by modern critics of undue subservience and disgraceful boot-licking are not borne out by his poems. Domitian undoubtedly suppressed with ruthless vigor the orators and historians of the opposition. The fifteen years of silence, so bitterly recorded by Tacitus, did not, however, apply to literature in general, certainly not to poetry. Quintilian received consular honors at the hands of Domitian and poetry contests flourished. Martial was already attracting some notice even before the day of Domitian. His first publication, the *Book of the Spectacles*, made use of the

Flavian Amphitheater (the Colosseum) to exhibit the facile cleverness of the young man from Spain. A modernized version of the
opening trifle is perhaps excusable if only to give an idea of the
tone.

> The pyramids are now old stuff
>   As dated as the horse-car;
> Diana's temple's not enough
>   To win another Oscar;
> The Hanging Gardens' day is done,
>   They're strictly eo-Asian:
> For seven wonders we have one—
>   The Bowl of T. Vespasian.

Flattery, yes, but in the best manner of a modern newspaper commentator. Incidents of the performance evidently gave a chance
for something more extreme.

> The elephant salutes on bended knee
> That chased the frightened bull a moment since:
> No trainer, Caesar, taught him flattery—
> Even an elephant salutes our Prince.

The charges of cringing mendicancy are of course based on
later poems in which Domitian is hailed as a god. Two comments
are pertinent. Our opinion of Domitian is largely determined by
hostile evidence and, while his cruelty and despotism is well at-
tested so far as the aristocratic opposition is concerned, we have
no evidence that the populace, appeased by bread and the circus,
found him to be the embodiment of wickedness. Also there is need
to remind ourselves that the established custom of patronage did
not lower the status of the worthy recipient. Later on, when Martial retired from Rome, Pliny helped him with his expenses and
was pleased with himself for this to the extent of publicising his
act. "I hear," he writes to a friend, "that Valerius Martial is dead
and I grieve to hear it. He was a man of intellectual ability, keen
and spirited, one who in his writings had an abundance of wit and

sting and no less straightforward integrity. I helped him, when he went into retirement, with his travelling expenses. I did this as a token of our friendship and also as an acknowledgement of the verses which he wrote about me." It is worth while quoting the verses which Pliny acknowledged. In them there is no cringing servility but rather the banter of a real friend with a nicety of teasing which was perhaps not obvious to the somewhat pompous barrister. (X.19.)

> This little book with laughter mocking
> Nor proper quite yet not too shocking,
> Thalia, take in its new dressing
> And give to Pliny with my blessing.
> Your way lies up Subura's alley
> Where you can see, above my valley,
> Standing adrip within his fountain
> Old Orpheus charming from the mountain
> The marvelling beasts, the Phrygian eagle
> And Ganymede, the bell-boy regal.
> Next, your friend Pedo's humble dwelling,
> Then Pliny's home with wisdom welling.
> But do not at an hour unseemly
> Go knocking at that door supremely
> Proper. Through long, long days he labors
> To serve Minerva while the neighbors
> Marvel at briefs whose learned pages
> Shall stun the court till future ages
> Compare them with the inspired fury
> Of Cicero before the jury.
> Night is your time when lamps are lighted
> And Bacchus rules and wit's excited,
> When frenzy all the soul immerses
> And even grim Catos read my verses.

Whether the *Liber Spectaculorum* was responsible or not we cannot say but at least as early as the following year Martial received a definite mark of imperial favor. He was given the privileges accorded by law to the fathers of three children and this in spite of the fact that he was a confirmed bachelor. His recognition of the favor (II.92) is typical of Martial's ability to smile at himself and it is certainly far from cringing.

> He gave me (I requested it) the rights
> That go with children three. 'Twas the reward
> Which he alone could give my humble muse.
> Farewell to marriage. I will not be said
> To have wasted wantonly my prince's gift.

Martial's early muse was indeed humble. Aside from the skits on the circus games (80 A.D.) we have a very considerable number (500) of what may be called cracker mottoes. These are trifles to go with dinner favors or Saturnalia presents. But he must have been writing epigrams and circulating them for some time for Books I and II which seem to have been published together came out in 86 and contain nearly two hundred epigrams carefully composed and thoroughly polished.

The introductory epigram in Book I opens a question which may well be faced before considering the poems as a whole. Almost all critics of Martial discuss either scathingly or apologetically his indulgence in obscenity. H. E. Butler *(Post-Augustan Poetry)* is the most extreme in his condemnation of the poet. After stating that his erotic epigrams do not for the most part rise above the pornographic level and that Martial also reveals an infinite capacity for cringing or impudent vulgarity in his peevish mendacity, Butler goes on to speak of his "almost unparalleled obscenity." Martial undoubtedly invited a charge (not perhaps so violent as Butler's) when he wrote the introductory poem for his first volume of general epigrams.

> The games of Flora well you know,
>> The lewd carouse, the jesting rough.
> Why came you, Cato, to the show?
>> To make your exit headline stuff?
> I want no Catos at my play
>> But if they come, why let them stay.

And again much later in life he defended himself with the old commonplace which even Ovid had made use of, that while his lines might be lewd his own life was pure. (XI.15.)

> I've written poems that Cato's wife
>   Or any Sabine mother
> Could read throughout a pious life
>   With husband or with brother.
>
> But this book's for the carnival,
>   A riot first and last;
> It shall with drunken madrigal
>   Forget the prudish past.
>
> Twill sport with boys, with maidens toy,
>   Nor blush to call to mind
> What 'tis that fills the world with joy
>   And likewise with mankind.
>
> I'll emulate the barnyard cock
>   As Numa did of old;
> So blame the season for your shock:
>   *My* morals are pure gold.

It is hardly necessary to point out the Roman addiction to coarse humor and frank expression of sexual affairs, decent and otherwise. But to condemn a satiric epigrammatist as almost unparalleled in the field is to be blind to the same element in the hendecasyllables of Catullus, the satires of Horace and Persius and Juvenal and in fact in a considerable portion of Latin literature. A difference from our point of view is beyond question, but Martial, extreme and often to us disgusting, is far from unique in this regard and only a horrified and naive Puritanism can seriously conclude that he was himself a repulsive beggar or a lewd wanton.

The epigram in Greece was inscriptional in origin. With their poetical sensitivity and their practical ingenuity the Greeks had early developed the elegiac inscription which gave in a few couplets, or even in one, the idea which was most important and relevant to the situation. The Roman was more given to inscribing facts on a tombstone or statue and resorted to abbreviations rather than to poetry. But the new poets found the elegiac couplet convenient for expressing their personal feelings and thoughts and, while they did not use the term, they introduced the epigram into Latin literature. Catullus' short elegiacs deal largely with his personal reactions to individual persons or incidents. Martial claims Catullus as his earliest model but his emotions are far more controlled than Catullus' and he is definitely more interested in the neatness with which an idea may be expressed. In addition, Martial had absorbed the satiric spirit and his epigrams have a quality foreign to the earlier product, a quality composed of the urbanity, the saltiness and sting, which characterized the best satires of Horace. Each epigram expressed one idea identified with a single individual or incident and so inevitably tended to produce a "point" which characteristically emerged as a surprise in the last line or even in the last word. Hence the modern conceit that an epigram is like a bee—short and sweet with a sting in its tail.

> Chloe raised a handsome tombstone
>> To her husbands, three times two,
> On the stone wrote *Chloe fecit*:
>> What more simple, what more true? (IX.15.)

Martial was by no means, however, an imitator. He recognised generously, as had Horace, the originator of the form which he had adopted but he freely extended and varied the form and through it expressed his own ideas and fancies. His epigrams have much the same range as Horace's satires as well as that of Catullus' *nugae* and the objects of his raillery are closely akin to those of Juvenal's vituperation: the frantic confusion of the city, the indignities of the patron-client relationship, the worship of money, the viciousness of women, the low estate of poetry. But Martial had not the sustained wrath of Juvenal; his attacks are tempered with wit and his philosophy of life is one of moderation. The Stoicism which he admires is the same as that which Tacitus commended in his father-in-law Agricola. He was moved by the heroism of a Paetus Thrasea and even more by that of Arria but his highest admiration was reserved for the moderate Stoic. (I.8.)

> Because you serve the creed that Cato served
> But in such fashion as to guard your life
> Nor rush with naked breast on naked swords
> To win a martyr's crown, I count you great.
> Not him I praise who buys cheap fame with death
> But him who wins our plaudits—and survives.

It comes therefore as no surprise when we find Martial again and again expounding the Horatian theme, *carpe diem*. (1.15.)

> Good old Julius, first of all
>   My friends, sedate or jolly,
> Sixty years you've lived this fall
>   Nor known an hour of folly.
>
> Don't put off what fortune's finger
>   May erase forever:
> Troubles last and labors linger,
>   Joys and pleasures never.
>
> Grasp them as they pass your way
>   Or lose them to your sorrow.
> Live to-day, man, live to-day:
>   Too late to live to-morrow.

This theme he develops even more carefully in an epigram addressed to Quintilian, the great rhetorician and teacher of the day. He neatly suggests the whole argument of Horace's first satire, that men stick to uncongenial lives because they are swayed by the desire for wealth and prestige. Then, again like Horace, he states his own humble desires. (II.90.)

Quintilian, guardian of our wayward youth,
    Glory of Rome, her present and her past,
Because I thirst for life nor hide the truth
    I crave indulgence: none can live too fast.

Let him put off life's joy whose only aim
    Is to surpass the wealth in Croesus' halls
Or whose grim pride is that ambiguous fame
    Ancestral portraits lend to atrium walls.

For me a blackened hearth, a spring to rise
    Bubbling and cold, broad meadows brown with hay,
Contented slaves, a wife that's not too wise,
    By night sound sleep, no quarreling by day.

It is worth noting incidentally the careful construction of his simple epigram. The first stanza implying a thirst for Life with a capital L; the alternative, postponement of a joyous life in order to pile up wealth or win to high position; then the statement of the simple life which he really craves. It would be ridiculous to claim for Martial any real devotion to simple country life, but he cannot be truly understood unless we recognise that one part of his nature did long for the peace which he could not find in the city. When he wrote Epigram II.38 I suspect that Linus stood for a considerable element of Rome's population in Martial's mind.

Linus, you ask what good my farm can do:
    It saves me, Linus, from the sight of you.

Perhaps it was always more disgust with the mad confusion and garish cheapness of Rome than love of real country life which possessed him. When, somewhere about 87, he broke away from the city life and went to Cisalpine Gaul, he implies as much in an introductory poem to his third book. (III.4.)

Off to Rome, my book, and say
    If they should ask you whence
That you have trod the Aemilian Way
    Two hundred miles thence.

And if they ask you why I stay
    Your answer's but a word:
He'd rather stay from Rome away
    Than run with such a herd.

When comes he back? perchance they'll ask:
    He left, a poet, you'll answer,
He'll come again in comic mask
    When he's learned to be a dancer.

But he *did* return and he endured the life at which he railed for
ten years more and then went back to Bilbilis for the last five years
of his life. He had some sympathy with his hypothetical hero,
Tuccius: (III.14.)

Tuccius came to Rome to live
    All the way from Spain
But when he found what Rome could give
    He went to Spain again.

Martial must have been sixty years old when he wrote from
Spain to Juvenal contrasting the life of Bilbilis with that of Rome.
Sixty seemed older to a Roman than it does to us and Martial's
life had not been a restful one. Weariness may have had much to
do with his appreciation of the rustic life. There is however a
sincerity about this poem which seems to come from the heart. In
retirement the writer is thoroughly enjoying the country life which
has always been to him a shadowy ideal and enjoying it even
through an occasional pang of nostalgia for the nerve-wracking
pleasures of his younger days. (XII.18.)

While you with restless nerves, my Juvenal,
Climb feverish up Subura's cobbled way
Or mount Diana's tiring slope, the while
You call on this or that great socialite
Or sweat your way along the Caelian Hill,
Myself at peace, the years forgotten now,
My Bilbilis, though proud in proven gold,
Has taken back and made a man again,
A farmer too. I learn once more to turn
The heavy soil and twist my tongue about
The Spanish names, tougher than any soil.
And then I sleep—oh, what a joy is there—
I sleep with none to wake and pay myself
For all those twenty sleepless years in Rome.
No toga here; I wear what comes to hand,
Eat daily my own garden truck and know
My household even as I know myself.
So would I live and so, at last, I'd die.

Satirists always bewailed the sad estate of poetry and Martial exhibits the same attitude with his own particular emphasis: poetry doesn't pay. (I.76.)

Flaccus, thou darling of my heart,
    Reward of all desire,
Why waste your time playing a part
    Amongst the Pierian choir?

What would you from Apollo's *love*?
    Minerva's *cash* is best:
She lends to all the gods above
    At deadly interest.

Why, pray, the *wreaths* of Bacchus don?
    Minerva's tree bears *fruit*.
Save weeds and water, Helicon
    Can offer you no loot.

Think you the Muses passing fair?
  The forum's rich and near:
There's wealth—the poet's passing rare
  That rates a feeble cheer.

The urbane irony is worthy of the best satirist but the bitterness was sincere and comes out more openly in V.56.

Lupus, you ask in harried doubt
  What trade to give your hopeful.
Well, first, all literature is out:
  No Cicero or Vergil

To-day could make an honest cent;
  Disown him if he's highbrow.
But if he seems on money bent
  Then have him play the oboe.

If that's beyond his I.Q. rate
He still can turn to real estate.

Finally, the poet gives to his friend and patron Flaccus his theory of why poetry is at a low ebb. (VIII.56.) The epigram is often cited as indicative of Martial's undignified and shameless mendicancy. It is a matter of individual judgment as to whether the tone is subservient or that of a friend, free to take a certain liberty. At any rate the epigram is carefully done, *con amore*.

The while our grandsires' age yields place
  To our more ample size
And Rome grows greater with her Lord,
  You, Flaccus, show surprise
That we have yet no Vergil's voice
  To sing war's panoplies.

Do you provide Maecenases,
  The Maros will appear

And your own countryside produce
    A Vergil singing clear.

For he, a Tityrus in tears,
    Had lost his humble keep;
From poor Cremona banished, he
    Was tending strangers' sheep.

The Tuscan smiled and thrust aside
    Rude poverty and hard,
Bade them begone. Take wealth, he said,
    Take wealth and be a bard.

Straightway *Italia* Vergil cried,
    Arma virumque too,
Who scarce before with trembling voice
    Had sung his *Culex* through.

Why talk of Marsus, Varius,
    And every glorious name?
Shall I become a Vergil straight
    Your goodness to proclaim?
I'll never be a Vergil, no:
    But I *might* beat Marsus' fame.

Surely Martial had Horace in mind and he had much of
Horace's benevolent outlook on life. Perhaps it was the lack of a
Maecenas that kept him from being wholly Horatian. Like the
Augustan satirist he insisted that his subject was contemporary life
in its realistic aspect. (X.4,7–10.)

Why fashion empty tales from dreary myths?
Read here what life admits is wholly hers.
No centaurs here you'll find, no gorgons here,
No Harpies: *man's* the subject of my page.

Again, like Horace, he had his own ideal of a simple and satis-

fying life but he expressed it in terms of an experienced realist.
(X.47.)

> What makes life worth the entrance fee?
> I'll tell you, sir, take this from me.
> Some not too grimly gotten dough,
> Enough to eat, somewhere to go;
> No lawyer's fees, no social stew,
> Clean bill of health and time to do
> The things I like; some honest friends
> Of jovial tastes; a board that lends
> Simple content, from ructions free;
> A gentleman withal I'd be;
> Sound sleep to speed the night away,
> Sound peace of mind to truly say
> I neither fear my final day
> Nor long to have it come my way.

Satire then and the spirit of satire had much to do with the
outlook of Martial and the tone of his verse. Happily it was as
much the satire of Horace as that of Juvenal. Martial had absorbed the satiric spirit of his century but to a considerable extent
he had escaped its bitterness. This quality of bitterness appears
more often in the epigrams which conform most strictly to the
type which Martial ascribes to Catullus. But in these shorter and
more bitter epigrams it is the pungent wit which predominates
rather than the sheer bitterness or vindictive rage. This is clear in
his fling at the doctors (I.47).

> Diaulus, once a doctor brave,
>   Is now a brave mortician.
> There's no real change: still to the grave
>   He sends them on commission.

Or at the lawyers (VI.19).

My case deals not with homicides
    Of any class whatever;
My stolen nanny goat resides
    Within my neighbor's cellar.

The judge demands some proof and you
    Expound the tale of Cannae,
The Mithridatic struggle too
    And all the miscellany

Of hero's deeds from Marius
    To Mucius and to Sulla
In mighty tones and endless fuss
    With dignity and color.

Postumus, please, one word devote
To my poor stolen nanny goat.

By this method Martial accomplishes about as much in six pregnant lines as Juvenal had with a complete and detailed satire on Virro. In attacking Caecilianus he strikes at the boorish snob who serves two menus at his table. (I.20.)

Tell me, Caecilianus, are you sane?
With all your guests to watch, you only eat
The dainty mushrooms from the hills of Spain.
What wish for that huge gullet so replete?
I know: I pray the gods it be your fate
One day to eat the kind that Claudius ate.

Caecilianus was the target of a more general attack many years later. (IX.70.)

"O tempora, O mores" Tully cried
    When Catiline hatched his conspiracy,
When citizens in myriads had died
    By Pompey's sword and Caesar's tyranny.

To-day, Caecilianus, why do you
   "O tempora, O mores' " still exclaim?
To-day there is no civil war to rue:
   Your "mores" give the "tempora" their name.

Occasionally the victim is anonymous either because he will be readily recognised by the reader or because the attack is extreme and might lead to legal action if made precise. Epigrams II.71 and II 73 will illustrate the two types of poems without personal address.

When I recite my verses
   You counter with some lines
From Marsus or the curses
   Catullus' wit refines.

I know you do it kindly
   To prove how much the best
Are mine. Be still more kindly:
   Recite your own, you pest.

* * * * *

No bounder in the town of Rome
   Will touch your ugly wife.
While she, unmarried, dwelt at home
   She led an untempted life.

But now you put a hundred guards
   About her and the blades
Come prowling round like lustful pards:
   Your genius never fades.

More pleasant from our point of view are the poems in which Martial expresses his devotion to his real friends, of whom Julius Martial seems to have been the closest. He was somewhat older than the poet and obviously well-to-do. His home on the Janicu-

lum inspired one of Martial's finest poems and his closest approach
to the lyric. (IV.64.)

Ye humble acres calling Julius lord,
Yours is a homestead happier far than those
Renowned Hesperides. Atop the long
And lazy summit of Janiculum,
Where sun and shadow etch deep terraces,
The wooded ridge swells gently and enjoys
A fairer heaven; and when the clouds descend
To hide the curving valleys, it alone
Shines with its own clear light. The delicate
Roof lines rise silent toward the purer stars.
Thence you may look upon the Seven Hills
And hold all Rome within a single glance,
The Alban Mount, the slopes of Tusculum,
And all that lies cool on the city's skirts;
Ancient Fidenae, little Rubrae, and
The fruitful grove that boasts the maiden blood
That once Anna Perenna shed. Beyond,
The traveller moves along the Flaminian Way
Or passes neath the old Salarian Gate
In soundless chariot whose far off wheels
Shall never break your slumbers, nor the shouts
Of sailor or of bargeman though so near
The Mulvian Bridge and at your very feet
The boats slip swiftly down the Tiber's stream.
This home within the city yet remote
Its master perfects till you think tis all
Your own, so ungrudging is the courtesy
Of his fine welcome. Ye who scorn all things small,
Go farm cool Tibur with a hundred shares,
Conquer Praeneste, make one vast estate
Of high-perched Setia, hanging from the sky.
Rather than all of these I choose as mine
The humble acres calling Julius lord.

Martial rallies Julius (in I.15, already quoted) on his conservative manner of life, urging him to taste its joys before it is too late, but there is never a question of the poet's real affection for his wealthy friend. If there were any doubt it would be dispelled by III.5 which went with his book to Julius from Gaul.

> Venturing without me to the mighty town,
> My little book, to many or to one
> Would'st take my commendation? One's enough,
> One who'll not treat you as a stranger waif:
> Julius, the name that's ever on my lips.
> Just past the pillars of the colonnade
> Where Daphnis lived, where Julius lives to-day.
> His wife will take you to her hands and heart
> And welcome you, dust covered though you come.
> And if you see or him or her you'll say:
> "Your Martial greets you." Say no more than that.
> Strangers need commendation. I would not
> Commend myself to those who are my own.

This poem should be compared with that which went with the tenth book to Pliny (X.19, already quoted). Both are friendly but there is definitely a warmth in the address to Julius which was not evident in the one to Pliny.

An interesting group of Martial's friends may be reconstructed from his invitation to a simple but obviously congenial party. (X.48.). The first named guest is Arruntius Stella, the poet to whom Statius dedicated his first book of Silvae and for whose wedding he wrote an epithalamium (Silvae, I.2). Nothing is really known about Stella's poetry. He was a man of wealth and position, consul in 101 A.D. Martial associates him (IX.55) with Flaccus as among his rich friends and patrons. The tone of this and other epigrams to these two men indicates not only generous patronage but an easy friendship, almost intimacy. One appeal to Flaccus already quoted (VIII.56) is particularly nice from a literary point of view. Cerialis seems to have been a man of small means like Martial who elsewhere invites him to a meal about which he says that he will lie and make it sound like one of Stella's dinners if that will induce Cerialis to come. Also, he will let his guest recite his own poetry at any length. Canius too evidently wrote poetry but was best known as a merry story teller. About Lupus little can be said. He gave Martial a *rus sub urbe,* a suburban farm so small that the poet would have preferred to change one letter and have a *prandium* instead of a *praedium* of this sort. The epigram (XI.18) was published from Spain after Martial had left Rome permanently and is elaborately clever, so much so as to arouse some doubt as to its interpretation. Something of the same might be said of the epigram (also to Lupus) which gives the bitter advice about a son (V.56, already quoted). Lupus' place at this friendly table is still a puzzle but the group is typical—rich and poor but all with some interest in poetry and all of a definitely social bent.

The eighth hour sounds from Isis' noisy shrine,
    The guard is changing with great show of haste.
Too hot at three, at four the baths are fine,
    (At two they boil to suit Neronian taste).
So come, my Stella, Nepos, Canius,
    And Cerialis come and Flaccus too.
The table's ready set for seven of us,
    So bring along Lupus with the rest of you.
My steward's wife, to whet our appetite,
    Has sent in mallows and the choicest crops
My garden bears: lettuce and leeks. To-night
    We'll have some mint as well and onion tops,
Smoked fish with eggs to garnish, salted tripe
    Will finish the hors d'oeuvres. One course beside
Should serve, a kid snatched from the wolf, with ripe
    Succulent beans and sprouts, the garden's pride.
For choice, a chicken or the remnant ham
    Survived from yesterday. Desert shall be
The finest apples and, to wash them down
    Nomentan wine, my own, the flagon free
From dregs, filled when Frontinus ruled the town.

> Then gossip, but no scandal whose import
> Brings shame to-morrow for what's said to-night.
> My table brings no diner into court.
> *We'll* match the chances of the green and white.

Martial's attitude toward Silius Italicus is somwhat different. Silius was a man of high position and serious outlook on life. Martial had little liking for conventional epic such as Silius wrote but perhaps the historical type of epic appealed to him more than the mythological. At any rate there is real respect (hardly, I think, the sycophancy which has been charged) in his tribute to Silius. (IV. 14, already quoted in Chapter IX.)

A wholly new tone appears in the verses which Martial addresses to his good friend Pudens, a centurian in active service. The allusions are obvious, the atmosphere hearty. When Pudens married Claudia Peregrina, Martial celebrated the occasion with an epigram (IV.13) fulsome enough for any top sergeant but also robustly sincere. The elm and the vine, the lotos and the water, myrtle and the shore, they are all there and the poem concludes:

> Fair Concord, stay thee on their bed
>   And Venus, leave them never.
> May she love him when youth has fled
>   Yet seem eighteen forever.

And so when Pudens goes off on a campaign to the far north, his poet friend is straightforward and simply sincere. (VI.58).

> And the gray dames spin not my fate
>   In threads of sombre hue,
> May we both live to celebrate
>   A knighthood won by you.

Tactfully he suggests to Pudens that he select the epigrams in Martial's books which he personally likes without a suggestion that the centurion might find many of them beyond his comprehension. (IV.29.)

A surfeit, Pudens, spoils the taste
    Of readers: stick to samples.
Tis rarity that wins; I haste
    To prove it by examples.

The earliest fruit, the Spanish rose
    Have each the perfect flavor;
The wench that does not all disclose
    At once retains her savor.

More connoisseurs read Persius' book
    Than Marsus' many volumes:
So at my verses take a look
    And choose your favorite columns.

One more associate may be mentioned, one who was evidently
a generous patron as well as a loved friend. In Epigram VIII.45
Martial neatly combines a welcome home to Terentius Priscus with
a compliment to Flaccus.

Flaccus, from Aetna's shore, oh happy day,
    Safely Terentius Priscus comes at last.
Open the jar that for this holiday
    Has waited while a hundred consuls passed.

What other night so fair shall grace my home?
    Or good wine warm our hearts more fittingly?
Only when Cyprus sends *you* back to Rome
    Shall joy again burst forth unstintingly.

Comfortably settled on his farm in Spain, Martial dedicated his
twelfth and last book to Priscus and with it a short epigram ac-
knowledging the favors which this patron had bestowed on him.
It has no great warmth of feeling but it does indicate a proper
dignity on the part of the recipient of patronage and a real sense
of gratitude without subservience.

Maecenas, knight of Tuscan line,
    Gave what it takes to Varius,
Bade Vergil and his Horace dine
    And cease their life precarious.

Loquacious Fame and parchment partial
    Shall tell the world, Terentius mine,
That you have done the same for Martial,
    Giving me genius, wit—and wine.

If Juvenal was the scourge of his day, Martial was its commentator. To him not everything in life was bad: some things were good (especially friends), some outrageous, some merely ridiculous. For all of them he had his comments ready and, like any first class columnist, he had for each the appropriate approach. He was not—he never claimed to be—a great or inspired poet but he had the gift of illuminating the trivialities of an age of which he himself was a vital part and in so doing to make it vivid to his readers for all time to come.

Epilogue

Time has crystalised certain popular generalisations about the century covered by the ten writers who have been the subjects of discussion in this volume. The Julio-Claudian "dynasty" has become the dark age of tyranny, the Flavian era one that brought relief with practical common sense, only to revert into depths of oppression under the monster Domitian, and finally to be replaced by the sunlight and happiness of the Ulpian regime. Scholarly research has corrected many a misapprehension involved in this picture, shown to have been the fruit of biassed reporting. But the corrections have not resulted in complete revision and the surviving literary products of the century reflect in general something of the traditional conception of the atmosphere which prevailed in each successive period of the century. The reign of Tiberius saw the last flicker of that explosive surge of creative genius which we know as the Augustan Age, to be followed by a retreat into philospohy or rebellion in the days of Nero. The Flavian era produced a mixed product: in part the result of a divorce of poetry from reality, a retirement into the ivory tower, in part a violent revolt against the realities of a changing society. Finally, with the advent of the Ulpian emperors, came a partial return to the freer creative atmosphere of the lost days of the Augustan Age. Trajan was no Augustus nor was he blest with a Maecenas. Martial had written in Epigram VIII.56:

> Do you provide Maecenases,
>> The Maros will appear
> And your own countryside produce
>> A Vergil singing clear.

Perhaps, but there must be available Vergils if this happy result is to eventuate.

That much was expected of Trajan there can be no doubt, but the expectations must have been more keenly felt in the area of historical prose than in the field of poetry. Tacitus wrote with obvious sincerity: "Now at last our spirit is returning and, although at the very beginning of this most happy age Nerva Caesar has combined elements once wholly incompatible, imperial power and freedom, and although Nerva Trajan is daily increasing the happiness of our time until the public confidence has conceived not only hope but strong faith in that hope, nevertheless, by the nature of human weakness, remedies are slower than disease." Such confidence on Tacitus' part produced his great Histories and Annals.

Martial too, though he had been less constrained than Tacitus under Domitian's censorship, expressed relief and new hope with the change of dynasty. Nerva was the kindliest of princes under whom all Helicon could rejoice; just and benevolent rule had returned and fears were banished. (XII.6.) Rome, the mistress of the world, could now invite the barbarian beyond the pale to come and behold a real Caesar. (XII.8.) And finally Martial addressed Trajan directly (XII.9.) telling him of the happiness in Spain under the governor he had sent there and expressing the thanks of the province to the emperor for sending them a man of his own character.

All very well. But the springs of original genius seem to have been too deeply buried under the silt of rhetoric and satire for even the most benevolent sponsor to be able to restore them quickly to the world. And Trajan was busy fighting, Hadrian travelling. Some day there would be a new flowering of Latin poetry. The first intimation of this and of what it might be like appeared in that astounding poem which Walter Pater made familiar, the "Vigil of Venus". This unique specimen of Latin poetry was probably written late in the second century. The first impulse of the critic is to say that it is wholly un-Roman but this is to overlook two characteristics of "The Vigil". The meter shows a strong tendency to return to the old Italic accentual verse and the romantic tension has a strong affiliation with the passionate tone of Lucretius in his tribute to Venus nearly three hundred years before. And both Lucretius and the author of "The Vigil" associate the romance of Venus with the advent of spring.

It is quite true that in our modern tradition it is conventional for the young man's fancy to turn to love in the spring of the year, but such was not so clearly the case with the Latin poets. In Catullus, spring is a date, the time when he is released from an uncongenial assignment in Bithynia. In Lucretius, as noted above, spring did arouse thoughts of love but tradition attributed the product of these thoughts to a love potion and labelled him mad. To Vergil, spring is the time of planting and of renewed life in field and garden. To Horace, spring marks the time for congenial drinking parties in the country. But in the "Vigil of Venus", spring with all its romance bursts upon us in unrestrained passion.

> The young spring, the singing spring, in the spring
>   the earth was born:
> Who has loved shall love again and he who never
>   loved shall love.

It is a new realm of poetry far removed from the environment of Seneca and Juvenal and even Martial. The world was not ready for it, only vaguely hopeful.

Appendix

Juvenal

III

The City of Rome

Distressed as I must be to lose a friend
Long tried, I can but envy one who goes
To fix his home at idle Cumae, thus
Adding one neighbor to the Sibyl's shore.
There is the gate to Baiae, a retreat
All loveliness. And even Prochyta
Is better than Subura, for what waste
Of solitude, what wretched spot of earth
Would you not welcome rather than endure
Daily the fear of fire or the collapse
Of buildings and the dangers numberless
That haunt the city, or the droning poets
Reciting in the dogdays? But the while
His household goods entire were being piled
On one small wagon, by the dripping arch
That spans the Capena Gate, Umbricius stood
And waited. There where ancient Numa once
Kept assignations with Egeria,
The sacred spring, the grove, the hallowed shrine
Are rented out to jews who come in herds
With picnic baskets. Every tree must yield
Its profit while the ejected Muses beg.
Down to the spring we strolled through curious caves
That Nature never wrought. How much more real

The presence of the nymph if nature's green
Margined the waters, and the native rock
Were undefiled by marble colonnades.
   At last Umbricius spoke: "Since in the town
There is no longer place for honesty
And no reward for toil; what yesterday
Promised is less to-day and will be less
To-morrow, I am off to where long since
Daedalus laid aside his weary wings.
While still not every hair is gray and while
Old age has yet to bend me and some thread
Remains for Lachesis to spin, before
My feet refuse to carry me without
Support, I'll leave my country. Catulus,
Artorius, let them live there and all
That can turn black to white, nor hesitate
To take the city contracts to repair
Rome's public buildings or collect the toll
By river bridge or harbor or to dredge
The sewers, conduct Rome's funerals and at last
Go bankrupt at a profit. These fine sirs
Were once the mountebanks blowing their horns
At country fairs who now give lavish games
And, when the crowd so wills, with downward thumb
Kill off the gladiators with a smile.
Then home to clean the munipical latrines.
Why not? For them it is that fickle Fortune
Lifts from the depths to place them at the top.
What can I do at home? I never learned
To lie. If someone's book is monstrous bad
I cannot praise it, ask it for a gift;
Astrology I never studied, hence
I cannot promise anyone the death
Of wealthy sire, nor would I if I could.
Frog's entrails are a thing I never saw.
Others may carry letters at a price
From mistresses to lovers or conspire

To consummate a theft. Not I, and so
No one will have me for a bosom friend,
As though a cripple with a withered hand.
Who's loved today who has not in his heart
Some guilty secret? None will make you friend
Or think himself your debtor if you know
Only what's good of him. *He's* Verres' friend
Who, when the impulse stirs, might bring to court
Fatal intelligence of Verres' past.
I tell you, not the golden sand that rolls
Down Tagus' stream is worth the sleepless nights,
The presents you dare not keep. The haunting fear
Of friends that hold you in relentless thrall.
 Who is it that wins the favor of our rich
And whom I chiefly flee? I will confess
Nor blush to tell: Oh, Romans, countrymen,
I cannot stand a Grecian Rome. And yet
What portion of our dregs is truly Greek?
Syrian Orontes has for many a day
Been emptying its bilge into our Tiber,
Bringing its speech and all its customs vile,
Its harps and pipes, its native tambourines,
Its girls for auctioning on circus days:
"Who'll buy a barbarian whore with turban gay?"
Quirinus, that stout farmer lad of yours
To-day wears a Greek dinner coat; around
His neck, perfumed of course, Greek garlands hang.
Yon fellow comes from lofty Sicyon,
That one from Alabandi; Amydon
Gave birth to this; another Samos bore,
Tralles or Andros; but each mother's son
Makes for the Esquiline or Viminal,
There to become the trusted confidante
Of our great blue-bloods—and their master too.
Quick is the Grecian wit, his boldness past
Control, his speech fluent as Isaeus' was.
What do you think him? Everything in one

He brings us: scholar, critic, robber, priest,
Circus performer, doctor, soothsayer too:
Yon hungry little Greek knows everything.
Tell him to climb to heaven: he'll make good.
For I am sure 'twas no Sarmation hero,
No Thracian nor a Moor that took to wings,
But one who first drew breath in Athens' streets.
Should I not flee their purple furbelows?
Shall he take precedence of me at court
Or dinner who arrived by cargo ship
At Rome, accompanied by prunes and figs?
Avails it naught that in my infancy
I ate the Sabine olive, breathed the air
Of Aventine? What if this fawning race,
Adept in flattery, praise the speech
Of ignoramuses, the face of one
Deformed, compares the emaciated throat
Of some sad invalid to the brawny neck
Of Hercules, raising Antaeus high
Above the earth, admires a squeaking voice,
Worse than a hen belabored by a cock.
All this I too might do but *them* the world
Believes. Or think you actors on the stage
Do better when they play the courtesan,
The wife, the slattern; you would swear by heaven
Each was a woman born, with woman's parts,
No actor counterpart. And yet in Greece
Peerless Antiochus would cause no stir
Nor even Stratocles, Demetrius
Or Haemus. Greeks are actors, every one.
You laugh: yon Greek shakes with a great guffaw;
He weeps if there's a tear in his friend's eye,
Yet without grief; if you should crave a bit
Of fire against the winter cold, he'll seize
At once his overcoat; if you remark
How warm the day, he'll burst into a sweat.
So we're no match; the better man is he

Who always, night and day, can mold his face
To others' looks, ready with loud applause
To greet a potent friend's successful belch,
A graceful urination or the gulp
That drains the golden goblet, bottoms up.
   Besides, his lechery knows no respect
Or fear: he threatens with obscene attack
Matron and maid, the beardless bridegroom too
And modest boys. If none of these be found
He brings to bed the granddame of his friend.
He would discover secrets of the house
To further blackmail. Since I've mentioned Greeks
Let's skip their lighter flights and listen to
Deeds of a greater scope. One stoic Greek
Killed his friend Barea with shrewd evidence.
Another, ripe in years, born in the land
That bred the Gorgonian nag, devised the death
Of his own ward. No tiny place is left
For any Roman where Protogenes
Or Erymanthus reigns or Diphilus
Who, true to type, will never share a friend,
Devouring him solo. For, when he has dropped
One little atom of his native poison
Into that ear, I am straightway removed
From the rich doorway and the long, long days
Of servitude are wasted. Nowhere else
Is clientship rewarded with such loss.
   Even without the Greeks what service pray
Can any poor man offer if before
The dawn, in full regalia, he presents
Himself, when praetors too urge on apace
Their lictors, knowing well the childless rich
Long since have wakened, fearing lest perchance
Their colleagues may outstrip them to salute
Albina first or Modia. Here the son
Of blue-blood parents acts as escort to
A rich man's slave who offers as a gift

To Catiena or Calvina more
Than legionary tribunes earn to win
The right to lie with her, while wretched you,
Attracted by the features of some whore,
Falter and quail to woo Chione's grace.
Say you at Rome give testimony true
As would be his of old chosen to receive
The Idaean Mother, say that Numa take
The stand to testify or he who saved
Trembling Minerva from the flaming fire:
At once the question's raised of patrimony
And the last thing that's weighed is character.
"How many slaves are his? How rich his fields?
How many platters grace his groaning board?"
Each man has credence in proportion strict
To moneys in his strong-box. *You* may swear
By all the gods of Rome or Samothrace:
The poor, they'll say, can fearlessly defy
The lightnings and the gods, for gods forgive.
And more than this, your very poverty
Gives all men food for jest, if your poor cloak
Is threadbare or your toga soiled or if
One shoe gapes open where the leather's torn
Or, crudely mended, shows a dozen scars
Held by coarse thread. Unhappy poverty
Has no more cruel sting than this: it makes
Ridiculous its victim. "Kick him out
If there be any shame" they say, "nor let
The man who lacks the cash sit in the seats
Reserved for knights. Put there the gilded sons
Of panders spawned in brothels; there the child
Of well dressed auctioneer shall give applause
And youths begotten in the training camp
Of gladiators, glossed with culture now."
Such is vain Otho's law, ranking us all.
What man is welcome now as son-in-law
Whose bank account is low, whose fortune bows

To his bride's fortune? What poor man to-day
Ever inherits? When will he be called
In counsel by the aediles? Long ago
The meagre citizens in solid ranks
Ought to have marched away. Not anywhere
Does he with ease rise from obscurity
Whose virtue lies concealed by poverty;
But here at Rome their fate is hardest: here
At mighty cost one hires a wretched room,
At mighty cost acquires a hungry slave
And eats a frugal meal at mighty cost.
Here you shall blush to eat from pottery
Which you would swear respectable if chance
Should spirit you away to live among
The Marsi or to grace a Sabine board
Where you would wear content Venetian wool.
   Did we admit the truth, the greater part
Of Italy ne'er dons the toga save
To grace the coffin. When some holiday
Hallowed by time returns and festive crowds
Throng the grass covered theater to behold
A favorite play, whose infants at the breast
Bellow in terror at the tragic work,
A common garb will mark the orchestra
And benches of the populace; to show
Their dignity even aediles are content
To don white tunics. Meanwhile here at Rome
Our dress outruns our wealth; the deficit
Is borrowed from another's bank account.
There is our dearest vice, for one and all
We flaunt our ostentatious poverty.
For, in the capital, there's not a thing
But has its price. What would you give just once
To greet great Corvus or some day to win
Veiento's silent, condescending nod?
A nabob shaves his beard for the first time
Or dedicates the severed baby curls

Of some too pampered slave, and celebrates
With calculating cakes which you may taste.
But, as you taste, remember this betimes:
We cringing clients must line the servile palm.
   Who ever at cool Praeneste or along
The wooded ridge of high Volsinii
Or in the simple towns of Gabii
Or Tibur, fears collapsing tenements?
Rome for the most part balances herself
Precariously on slender props installed
By agents whose ingenious artifice
Conceals the gaping cracks and bids us rest
In peace while dire catastrophe impends.
My mind's made up to live where neither fire
Threatens my peace nor terrors of the night.
Ucalegon shrieks "Water!" and removes
His few belongings; three floors burn below
And you lie ignorant. While panic reigns
The last to burn is he whose humble home
Only the tiles keep dry, up where the doves
Bestow their eggs. Codrus possessed a bed
Too small for Procula, six jugs to adorn
His simple sideboard and a drinking cup;
One ornament, a Chiron in repose,
One ancient chest of learned literature
Gnawed by barbarian mice. Who would deny
Codrus had nothing? Yet poor Codrus lost
All of that nothing. And the final blow
Falls when, thus stripped, he begs a crust and finds
None that will help him with a bite to eat
Or home to cover him. Yet if the mighty house
Of great Asturias has gone, the town
Wears mourning and the judge adjourns the court.
Then 'tis we groan at Rome's unhappy state,
Lament the evil chance. The fire still burns
While citizens come running with relief.
Money pours in, one sympathiser brings

A fair white statue in the nude, another
Contributes gems of Polycleitus' art
While some wise woman hastily bestows
The ancient trappings of the Asian gods.
Books and a bookcase speedily appear
Complete with a Minerva and a peck
Of solid silver. Persicus, the flower
Supreme of childless nabobs, furnishes
His house with rich donations far beyond
His losses till the whispering gossips say
He must have touched the conflagration off.

    If you can bear foregoing the circus games
Sora or Frusinone will provide
The best of homes for less than here you pay
To hire a hovel for a single year.
There you may have a garden and a well
Shallow and ample, making easy work
Of gardening while you fondly tend your flocks,
Steward of your own plot, that would supply
Pythagoras with a hundred ample meals.
Tis something, be it ever so remote,
To own an acre and be lord thereof.

    Here in the town the mightiest toll of death
Results from lack of sleep but sleeplessness
Is fostered by the undigested food
That clogs the weary stomach. Pray, what rest
Can rented lodgings give? A peaceful night
Demands a princely fortune. Rattling carts
In narrow alleys and the unholy shouts
Of cattle drivers would despoil of sleep
A Drusus or a sea-cow. If perchance
His social duties call, your rich man rides
High on the shoulders of his slaves. The crowd
Gives way before him while he takes his ease,
Reading or writing or gone fast asleep—
For the closed litter lures him to repose.
Yet he'll outstrip me: bustle as I will.

The crowd before me blocks the way, the wave
Following buffets me on every side.
An elbow digs my ribs, a litter pole
A swinging beam, a careless water jar
Batter my head, assailed from left and right.
Bespattered with foul mud and roughly kicked
By clumsy feet, at last a corporal's
Great hobnailed shoe assassinates my toes.
See you not what a murky cloud of smoke
Accompanies the morning calls? Each guest
A hundred of them, and a kitchen stove
Along with each. A Corbulo could scarce
Endure the burden of the pots and pans
Each wretched slaveling must negotiate
The while his running fans the expectant flame.
Tunics but newly pressed are rudely torn;
One passing dray carries a mighty fir
Swaying on high, the next a towering pine
Threatening our heads. And if the mountainous load
Of marble from another should upset
Upon the road, what of our bodies then?
Who would collect our bones? Gone like the breath
Of life is every victim from the herd
Of common folk. Meanwhile, all unconcerned,
His household scours the platters, pokes the fire,
Lays out the greasy strigils, flask of oil
And ample bath towel. While they bustle on
The master sits beside the Styx and views
With all the dread of a novitiate
The horrid ferryman with never a hope
Of passage o'er the muddy stream, poor man,
For none has put a penny in his mouth.
    Glance now at dangers of another sort,
The lofty buildings whence a broken pot
May crush your cranium as it hurtles down
From open window with an ample force
To dent the pavement. You would be a fool

Improvident to make your thoughtless way
To dinner without first making your will.
You face as many threats of instant death
As you pass windows and your only prayer
That they may be content merely to dump
The contents of their slop jars on your head.
    Your cutthroat, reeling drunken on the streets
Goes to a sleepless couch if he forsooth
Has found no victim. There like Peleus' son,
Mourning his dearest friend, tossing about
He thrashes endlessly, for there are men
Whom quarrels pacify. But insolence
Of youth or courage wrought by wine cannot
Betray him to attack the purple clad
Or those distinguished travellers attended
By able bodied slaves with torch and lamp.
But when the moon denies its rays to *me*
The ruffian scorns my humble candle light.
Behold the prelude of the wretched fight,
If fight it be with no resistance made.
He towers over you and bids you stand.
You must obey for, pray, what choice is yours
When he is mad who orders and, beside,
More powerful than you? "Where from" he cries,
Whose wine have you been swilling? What poor fool
Has shared his pauper's meal this night with you?
No answer? Tell me, on what beggar's mat
Can you be found or in what synagogue?"
Whether you answer or restrain your tongue
Tis all the same, he'll leave his mark on you.
Such is the liberty the poor man boasts:
The right to plead when beaten, to implore
Permission to retain what teeth are left.
Nor is this all. Robbers will halt you most
When shops are closed and every shutter fast.
Then is the heyday of the highwayman.
For they, as fishes to a safe preserve,

Flock to the city when the Pontine Marsh
And Gallinarian Wood are raided by
Our soldiery. What city forge to-day
Yields not its crop of chains? The greater share
Of all our iron turns to fetters now
Till rightly you may shudder lest ere long
There be no ploughs or mattocks in our fields.
Happy the sires of our great-grandfathers!
Happy the ages long since passed that saw
Even under kings *one* prison in all Rome.

 I am not done. The tale is endless, but
The mules are restless and the sun is low.
I must be off; the driver cracks his whip.
Farewell. Remember your old friend and when
Rome sends you to Aquinum for a rest
Invite me over to your hallowed shore
From my plain Cumae. If these irk you not,
I'll add more satires to this homely crop.

Juvenal

X

The Vanity of Human Wishes

In every land, from Gades in the west
To where the dawn breaks over Ganges, few
There be who can, free from the clouds of error,
Distinguish true good from its opposite.
What, with sound reason, do we fear or hope?
What do you ever undertake with such
Auspicious start that you do not repent
The issue of your act? Whole families
Complacent gods have wrecked through their own prayers.
Toga and uniform, pregnant with fate,
Men crave. The power of speech, high eloquence
Have proven fatal and the very strength
In which one put his faith has wrought his death.
Far more are strangled by the wealth compiled
With anxious care and bank accounts as much
Beyond all possible inheritance
As British whales outstrip our dolphins' size.
So in the direst days of Nero's reign
A full-strength cohort besieged Longinus' home,
The wealthy Seneca's great garden close
And the rich palace of the Laterans.
No soldiers search the hovels of the poor.
You may be carrying just a piece or two
Of common silver as you fare by night,
Yet you'll await in fear the sword and club,

Trembling at moon-cast shadow of a reed.
The empty handed traveller will sing
Right in the robber's face. The best known prayers
At every shrine are prayers for wealth, that our
Account may grow till it becomes the first
In all the forum. Yet no poison draught
Is drunk from pottery: fear *that* what time
You raise a jewelled cup or Setine wine
Glows in a golden goblet. Won't you then
Praise those philosophers of whom one laughed
Whenever he set foot outside his door
The other wept? The censure of a sneer
Is easy and the wonder, how such tears
Could ever flood the eyes. Democritus
Indulged in endless laughter though *his* town
Knew not our regal robes, our litters rich,
Nor yet our fasces nor our courts of law.
What if he'd seen the praetor reared aloft
Above the circus dust, in mighty car,
Wearing the Jovian tunic and the silk
Of Tyrian toga and the regal crown
Whose weight could not be borne by human neck?
(A sweating slave must carry it; his mate
Rides with the consul to deflate his pride.)
Now add the eagle on its ivory staff,
The trumpeteers, attendants in long line
And at his bridle citizens in white,
Their loyal friendship won by hoarded doles.
Yet, even in *his* day he found enough
To laugh at in each crowd, this wise old man
Whose wisdom taught that heroes of renown
Could come from sheep-brained races who were born
Beneath ill-omened skies. He laughed alike
At mankind's woes and joys and at their tears
And all the while mocked evil fortune's threats,
Pointing at her the finger of his scorn.

What *are* our prayers, then, vain or dangerous?
And for what blessings *should* we beg the gods?
Power political breeds jealousy,
Hurling its victims down: the glorious page
Of honors ends in ruin. Statues fall,
Ropes drag them off, the axes pulverise
The chariot wheels, the horses' innocent legs;
Now, now the fires roar, the bellows blow:
That head the people worshipped glows red hot:
Mighty Sejanus crackles. So there come
From that face, second in the whole wide world,
Jugs, slop-jars, frying pans and chamber pots.
Hang laurels on your door, lead the white bull
Up to the Capitol: Sejanus' self
Is dragged off by the hook for all to see.
Rejoicing everywhere. "Look at those lips;
Oh, what a face was that. Upon my word,
I never loved the man. But what the charge?
Who the informer? Who the witnesses?"
"Nothing like that. A weighty letter came
From Capri." "Fair enough: I ask no more.
But what of Remus' folk?" "They follow fate
As always, hate the man who's down. This folk,
If Nortia had preferred the Tuscan knight
And the old emperor, caught off his guard,
Had been the one to fall, at this same hour
Would hail Sejanus with Augustus' name.
Since we've no votes to sell, the State's no more
Concern to us. The citizen who once
Bestowed the imperial power, the fasces too,
The legions, everything, busies himself
Now only with himself, asks but two things:
Bread and the circus. "More, I hear, will fall."
"No doubt: the furnaces are big." "I thought
My friend Brutidius looked a little pale
Just now beside Mars' altar. I'm afraid

Our Ajax may demand some punishment
For poor support. Let's hurry to the bank
And give a lusty kick to Caesar's foe.
Make sure the slaves can see and can't deny
Or drag their trembling master off to court."
Such was the gossip, such the whispering
Over Sejanus. Would you then be hailed
As was Sejanus, have the self-same power,
Grant to this man the curule chair, to that
Command of armies, be the reputed guide
Of him who sits as lord on Capri's cliff
With his Chaldaean fortune-telling flock?
Of course you'd like to own the soldiery,
Those fine knights in the proud Praetorian Guard.
Why not? For even those who would not kill
Would like the power to kill. But what success
So glorious as to outweigh an equal share
Of miserable disaster? Would you choose
To don the mantle of this victim here
Rather than be a petty officer
At Gabii or Fidenae or dispense
Justice in market weights and, smashing all
The lying measures, clad in country clothes,
Be aedile at Ulubrae? Then confess:
Sejanus did not know the proper prayer.
For he who coveted high offices
And wealth inordinate was rearing high
A storied structure skyward whence to fall
With mightier ruin in the final crash.
What ruined Crassus and brought Pompey low
And that slave-driving lord, wielding the lash
On Roman citizens? I'll tell you, 'twas
The tyrant's power ruthlessly attained,
Answer of jealous gods to impious prayer.
Down to the son of Ceres with clean hands
Few kings and tyrants ever go in peace.

The famous eloquence of Cicero
Or of Demosthenes becomes the prayer
The schoolboy makes at every festival
While worshipping (one penny all he has)
Thrifty Minerva, while he still obeys
The slave who guards his little box of books.
Yet both these idols perished from eloquence:
The bursting flood of speech brought both to death,
Severed the hand and head of genius. But
The rostra never dripped with dullard's blood.
"Oh, happy Rome born in my consulship."
Had all his speech been such, great Cicero
Could well have scorned the swords of Antony.
I'd choose his silly poems to all the fame
The second great Philippic brought to him.
His too a cruel death whom Athens loved,
Impetuous as he held the guiding rein
Within the crowded theater. Sinister
His fate, born under angry gods; mere child,
His half blind father at the blazing forge
Working with fire and forceps, sent him straight
From Vulcan's anvil to the rhetor's school.

The spoil of war, trophies on tree trunks hung,
The bridle and the severed helmet strap,
The broken yoke and pole, the brazen beak
Of captured trireme, on the lofty arch
The humbled captive—these mankind believe
Boons more than mortal. It is these that tempt
Romna and Greek commanders and the wild
Barbarian chief, motives for endless risk
And toil. So far the thirst for fame outstrips
The thirst for virtue. Be there no reward,
What man woos virtue? Yet our country once
Collapsed before the glory of a few
And the consuming greed for praise and for

The inscription on the stone that marked their grave.
But that same stone one barren fig tree's strength
Could shatter when fate doomed the sepulchre.
Weigh Hannibal: how many pounds are left
Of that great general? Here lies the man
For whom not Africa was space enough,
Washed by the Moorish ocean, stretching out
From the hot Nile to the farthest tribes
Of Aethiopia with their elephants;
Spain joined his realm, he crossed the Pyranees;
Nature before him thrust the snow clad Alps:
He split the mountain crags with vinegar.
Already he holds Italy but still
He presses on. "For naught" he cries "is won
Until we crash the gates with Punic arms
To fix our standards in Subura's heart."
Oh, what a canvas there, fit for what brush:
Gaetulian beast bearing its one-eyed lord!
And what his end? Why, that same lord
(Oh, treacherous Fame) is conquered, headlong flees
To sit a suppliant at the palace gate
Of the Bithynian king till it shall please
The tyrant to awake. And so the end
Of that great spirit once confounding all
Affairs of earth is neither sword nor rock
But one small poisoned ring avenging all
The tragedy of Cannae. Madman, go
Charging the cruel Alps to make yourself
A tale for puling schoolboys to recite.
    One world was not enough for Pella's son:
The unhappy youth chafed at earth's narrow bounds
As though confined an exile by the cliffs
Of Gyaros or little Seriphus.
Yet when his arms have won the town beringed
With pottery walls he needs will be content
With one sarcophagus. Death only proves
How insignificant our little frame.

The world believes that Athos was o'ersailed
And all the fables lying Greece put forth
In ancient tale, that those same argosies
Passed on dry wheels over the bridge-bound sea,
That mighty rivers failed and every stream,
Drunk dry by Medes at table—all the myths
That Sostratos with sodden wings recites.
How looked he then, that bold barbarian,
When he returned from Salamis, whose wont
It was to lash the winds of heaven that ne'er
Had suffered such affront from Aeolus,
He who had bound the Shaker of the Earth
(Deeming it kindness not to brand the god—
For who could worship such divinity?)
How then did he return? A single ship
Ploughed with him through the bloody waves, made slow
By shoals of corpses. Such the price he paid
For glory granted his persistent prayer.

Give length of life, oh Jove, given endless years.
This is the prayer you pray, or well or sick,
Yet what continuous, overwhelming ills
Old age is heir to! First and foremost, see
That ugly, malformed face, unlike itself,
A hide for skin, long, hanging jowls
And wrinkles, like the grooves a mother ape
Graves in her offspring's face where Thabrica
Spreads wide her leafy groves. In youth, we know,
Variety's the law: one's handsomer
Than is another, one man's strong, another frail:
Old age is all one ilk. The voice that shakes
As shake the legs, as shakes the wobbling head;
The second infancy of dripping nose,
The munch of bread by gums untennanted,
Till he becomes a burden to his wife,
His children and himself that would disgust
Even a flatterer of Cossus' stamp.

His torpid palate relishes no more
The joys of wine and food. Forgotten now
The flame of love—if not forgotten, lost.
Look at another sense destroyed: what joy
For him in music of the lyre even if
Seleucus sings or other glittering star?
What matter where he's seated at the show
Who scarce can hear the horns or tuba's blast?
His boy must shout to make him hear the names
Of callers or to tell the time of day.
Scarce any drop of blood in his chill frame
That only fever warms, while round him dance
A chorus of diseases. Ask their names:
I'd sooner list the fools that Oppia loved,
How many patients Themison has killed
This autumn or the count of friends betrayed
By Baṣilus or wards that Hirrus robs,
How many men the slender Maura drains
In one short day, the list of followers
Corrupted by Hamillus. I could tell
More quickly what estates he owns to-day
Who was a barber when my flourishing beard
Declared my youth. For one, his shoulder hurts,
Another's legs are weak, another's hips,
Another, blind, envies the one-eyed man;
This one, with pallid lips, receives his food
At stranger's hand while he himself must gape
Before the banquet spread, with open mouth
Like baby swallow waiting for the worm
The fasting mother brings. Yet, worse by far
Than all these corporal ills, the failing mind
That soon forgets the names of slaves, the face
Of friend with whom he dined last night, of child
Whom he begat and reared. Tis then he writes
A cruel will, removing his own kin
And leaving all to Phiale to reward
The false breath of her seasoned harlotry.

If, on the other hand, his sense survive,
He still must face the funerals of his young,
Attend his loved wife's pyre, conduct the ashes
Of brother and of sister. Such the price
He pays for too long life, to see his home
Ever revisited by constant death,
Grow old in grief, wear mourning to the end.
The Pylian king, if Homer's word you'll take,
Was sample of a life well nigh as long
As any crow's. Happy, you say, because
He worsted death for generations, told
The tale of years by right hand digits' count,
And for a hundred autumns drank new wine.
I ask you for a moment to observe
His own resentment at the laws of fate
That stretched his thread of life, forced him to see
The burning beard of his Antilochus,
Asking of any friend that lent his ear
Why he must live so long, what he had done
So wrong that he must suffer endlessly.
The same was true of Peleus in his grief
For dead Achilles and of him as well
Who rightly mourned the shipwrecked Ithacan.
With Troy unscathed, Priam had gone below
To join Assaracus, Hector had borne
His ashes in procession to the tomb
And Hector's brothers, while the Ilian wives
Wept for their lord, the while Cassandra wailed
And with torn garments fair Polyxena,
Had he but died betimes, had died before
Paris had launched his predatory ships.
What boon his length of days? He saw
His whole world overthrown and Asia swept
By flame and sword. At last, his diadem
Abandoned, and his trembling body clothed
In soldier's uniform, he fell in death
Before the altar like an ancient steer

Spurned by the plow, yielding its scrawny neck
For slaughter to the sacrificial knife.
A man's death even so: his aged wife
Surviving him died like a snarling cur.
I hasten to *our* heroes and forget
The king of Pontus, pass by Croesus too
Whom Solon's eloquent wisdom bade await
The final stretch of his too lengthy days.
Twas too long life that brought imprisonment
And exile and Minturnae's marsh to him
Who, Carthage shattered, begged his daily bread.
For whom more blessed has nature e'er produced
Or Rome acknowledged, had he but breathed his last
Surrounded by his captives and the pomp
Of war, about to leave the chariot
Of his Teutonic triumph? Shrewdly wise
Campania gave to Pompey fever's boon;
But many cities with their public vows
Prevailed and so Rome's fortune and his own
Saved him to lose his head in sore defeat.
Such torturing end was not for Lentulus;
Cethegus too escaped such punishment
And even Catiline could die unmaimed.

Beauty of face and figure for her sons
With murmur soft, for daughters openly,
The anxious mother prays quite shamelessly
At Venus' shrine. "Why blame me, then" she says;
"Latona joys in her Diana's beauty."
But stay: Lucretia warns us not to wish
For loveliness like her's. Verginia
Would gladly give her beauty in exchange
For Rutila's humped back. But, likewise, sons
With too fair bodies wreck their parents' nerves
With constant worry: rare it is to find
Beauty and shame united. Granted, now,
The house be chaste as any Sabine home,

Teaching the purest morals; grant as well
That Nature with a lavish hand bestow
A character upright, countenance
Suffused with modest blood—what more can youth
Be given by Nature whose protecting power
Is better far than strictest guardian—
He'll never have a chance to be a man,
For prodigal corruption dares to tempt
Parents themselves, so bold is bribery.
No tyrant in his fastness ruthlessly
Castrates an ugly boy. Nero ne'er spoiled
A youth possessed of club foot or a hump,
No stripling with a paunch. Go now and gloat
Over your youngster's beauty which awaits
These dreadful dangers. He shall yet become
A famed adulterer, shall live in fear
Of every angry husband: he shall be
No happier in the outcome than was Mars
Albeit he fall not into Vulcan's net.
For there is vengeance beyond any law
For such offence: one victim plies the sword,
Another wields the bloody lash, and some
Have felt the horror of tradition's fish.
But your Endymion will of course despoil
Some matron whom he loves. Yet presently
As rich Servilia offers cash, he'll be
Her lover whom he loves not and accept
Her richest offering: what can any woman
Deny to rampant lust, whether she be
Oppia or Catulla? Women are one.
"But how can beauty harm the chaste?" you ask.
What profit to Hippolytus his stern
Resolve? Or to Bellerophon? She blushed
At his rejection as a woman scorned
And Sthenobeia's angry pallor showed
As white as Phaedra's: both took vengeance dire.
Never is woman such a savage beast

As when shame goads her hatred. What advice
Think you could sway the man whom Caesar's wife
Has willed to marry? He, the handsomest
And best of all patricians, wretched man,
Is carried away by Messalina's eyes
To his destruction. There the siren sits
Arrayed long since in wedding veil; the couch
Spread openly with purple coverlet
There in the garden; by the ancient rite
The dowry's set, a million sesterces;
The priest, the witnesses will come. Didst think
There would be secret rites, disclosed to few?
She'll have the legal best. Come, Silius,
What is your pleasure? If you'll not obey
You'll have to perish ere the lamps are lit:
If you consent to crime, there'll be delay—
A very little—till the tale, well known
To town and populace, shall reach the ear
Of Caesar, for his house will be the last
To hear of his disgrace. So come meanwhile,
Obey our orders, if a few days' life
Is worth the price. Whatever choice you make
Your fair white neck is destined for the sword.

   Shall men then pray for nothing? If you want
Advice from me, you'll leave it to the gods
Themselves to give what is expedient
For us and our affairs. The gods will grant
Not what is pleasant but most suitable.
Dearer to them is man than to himself.
We are led on by blind impulse or greed
To pray for wife or offspring but *they* know
What kind of wife 'twould be, what kind of sons.
But if you needs must make some prayer and bring
The entrails to the altar with your gift
Of blessed white pig sausage, then, I say,
Pray for a sound mind in a body sound.

Ask for a bouyant heart that fears not death,
That counts our span of life among the gifts
Of Nature, than can bear what toils may come,
That knows not anger nor too much desire,
That would prefer the toils of Hercules
To love and banqueting in Ninevah.

Index of Authors And Their Works